1950

The Handbook for Investment Committee Members

Founded in 1807, John Wiley & Sons is the oldest independent publishing company in the United States. With offices in North America, Europe, Australia, and Asia, Wiley is globally committed to developing and marketing print and electronic products and services for our customers' professional and personal knowledge and understanding.

The Wiley Finance series contains books written specifically for finance and investment professionals as well as sophisticated individual investors and their financial advisors. Book topics range from portfolio management to e-commerce, risk management, financial engineering, valuation, and financial instrument analysis, as well as much more.

For a list of available titles, visit our Web site at www.WileyFinance.com.

The Handbook for Investment Committee Members

*How to Make Prudent Investments
for Your Organization*

RUSSELL L. OLSON

WILEY

John Wiley & Sons, Inc.

Published by John Wiley & Sons, Inc., Hoboken, New Jersey.
Published simultaneously in Canada.

For general information about our other products and services, please contact our Customer
Care Department within the United States at 800-762-2974, outside the United States at
317-572-3993 or fax 317-572-4002.

Wiley also publishes its books in a variety of electronic formats. Some content that appears
in print may not be available in electronic books. For more information about Wiley
products, visit our web site at www.wiley.com.

Library of Congress Cataloging-in-Publication Data:

Olson, Russell L., 1933–
    The handbook for investment committee members : how to make prudent
investments for your organization / Russell L. Olson.
        p. cm.—(Wiley finance series)
    Includes bibliographical references and index.
    ISBN 0-471-71978-1 (CLOTH)
    1. Institutional investments—Handbooks, manuals, etc. 2.
Investments—Handbooks, manuals, etc. 3. Pension trusts—Investments. 4.
Endowments—Finance. I. Title. II. Series.
HG4527.046 2005
332.67'253—dc22

2004024099

Printed in the United States of America

10 9 8 7 6 5 4 3 2 1

*To Jeanette,
my wife
and my best friend*

Contents

Acknowledgments

This book is a much easier read—geared specifically for committee members—than my two prior books, *Investing in Pension Funds and Endowments: Tools and Guidelines for the New Independent Fiduciary*, published in 2003 by McGraw-Hill, and *The Independent Fiduciary: Investing for Pension Funds and Endowment Funds*, published in 1999 by John Wiley & Sons. Those books would be appropriate for a student or anyone who serves as an *adviser* to an *investment fund*. This book, for committee members, has been materially strengthened by input from several persons.

One is Joe Grills, former chief investment officer of the IBM retirement funds and currently serving on various investment organizations, such as the investment advisory committees of the state funds in New York and Virginia, and the boards of directors of the Duke University Management Company and selected Merrill Lynch mutual funds. Joe also is vice-chairman of the Montpelier Foundation and serves on the investment committees of two other endowment funds with assets between $120 and $150 million.

Another is Katherine Noftz Nagel of Masterwork Consulting Services. Kat has never served on an investment committee. Kat reviewed the manuscript from the standpoint of someone appointed to an investment committee for the first time, and she provided helpful suggestions as to what would make this handbook more helpful to someone who suddenly was asked to be a fiduciary.

Additional valuable input has come from Mike Manning, president of New England Pension Consultants, and two persons who happen to be attorneys—Jordan Sprechman, vice president and wealth advisor at J. P. Morgan Private Bank, and Edward Siedle, president of the Center for Investment Manager Investigations at Benchmark Financial Services, Inc.

Russell L. Olson

Introduction

Let's say I am a member of the investment committee of an endowment fund—for a college, hospital, museum, local Boy or Girl Scouts council, or my church or synagogue—or a member of the investment committee of a pension fund or foundation. Whether they've told me or not, I am a "fiduciary" for that organization. As such, what is my job? What is expected of me?

That's what this book is about.

Our job as a fiduciary is to act solely in the interests of our organization and, according to one definition, "to act with the care, skill, prudence, and diligence under the circumstances then prevailing that a prudent man acting in a like capacity and familiar with such matters would use in the conduct of an enterprise of a like character and with like aims."[1] That sounds heavy.

What qualifications are we expected to bring to this responsibility?

It is helpful if we are familiar with investments—to the extent that we participate in our employer's 401(k) plan, have an IRA account (Individual Retirement Account), or have other investments in stocks or bonds. We may even be a professional manager of common stock or bond investments, but that is certainly not necessary (and could, under some circumstances, be a drawback). Although investment sophistication helps, it is not a requirement for a committee member.

Neither we nor our fellow committee members are expected to be experts. One of the first responsibilities of a committee is to find an expert to rely on. If we have a very large fund, we may have a professional investment staff of sufficient competence on whom we can rely. If not, we should find a broad-gauged investment consultant on whom we can rely. If our fund is too small to afford a broadly knowledgeable consultant, we will need to rely on a member of our committee who has this experience and who would be competent and willing to serve in this capacity on a volunteer basis. Relying on an expert in whom we have confidence is a sine qua

---

[1]From ERISA (The Employee Retirement Income Security Act of 1974).

non, because we must recognize that we and our fellow committee members can't do it ourselves. And if we lose confidence in the expert we are relying on, we must get another.

If not investment expertise, then what criteria should a committee member meet? Here are some of the most important:

- High moral character, ready to avoid even the perception of a conflict of interest.
- Knowledge of how the fund relates to the financial situation of the plan sponsor.
- A healthy dose of common sense—the ability to reason in a logical manner, to apply abstract principles to specific situations, and to relate questions at hand to everything else we know.
- A flexible mind, willing and able to consider, weigh, and apply new concepts and ideas, and to challenge previously held concepts, including one's own.
- A willingness to accept a level of risk high enough to gain the investment return advantage of a long time horizon.
- A willingness to learn—about the kinds of concepts discussed in this book and about individual investment opportunities.
- An ability and willingness to attend all meetings of the investment committee and to do the homework before each meeting—to be prepared to discuss the subjects and proposals to be addressed at the meeting.

The purpose of this book is not to make anyone an investment expert—that's not necessary, or even realistic. The purpose is to help us understand information presented at committee meetings, to ask meaningful and productive questions, to evaluate the responses we receive, and to vote on recommendations knowledgeably.

ORGANIZATION OF THIS BOOK

We start in Chapter 1 with the functioning of our investment committee. In Chapter 2 we provide a primer on risk, return, and correlation—basic concepts in investing. Chapter 3 discusses the statement of Investment Policies that every investment committee should establish at the outset, and Chapter 4 covers how to put together a portfolio of asset classes. Chapter 5 serves as a reference about alternative asset classes. Then Chapter 6 deals with how to select and to monitor the investment managers or mutual funds that actually invest our assets. The importance of a competent custodian is covered in Chapter 7. Chapter 8 provides the kind of questions we might ask in evaluating the investment organization of an endowment fund, foundation, or pension fund.

Chapter 9 covers the structure of an endowment fund, the handling of restricted money in the fund, and the importance of using the Imputed Income method to calculate annual payments to the fund's sponsor. And Chapter 10 briefly summarizes what's different about a pension fund. Chapter 11 provides a brief summary of the book.

I have tried to make this book appropriate for both sophisticated investors and relative neophytes. One way I have done this is to place some of the more advanced concepts in boxes or in footnotes. This should allow someone with little investment background to comprehend the main information without reading them, while the more experienced investor may find interest there.

To make this book easier to read, I have taken four shortcuts you should be aware of:

Shortcut 1. All of this book applies to endowment funds and foundations as well as to pension funds. There are innumerable instances where I have referred to our "endowment fund, foundation, or pension fund," but instead of using those words, I have simply said our *investment fund* or simply our *fund*. Whenever you see these words in italics you should interpret their meaning as our "endowment fund, foundation, or pension fund." The similarities in managing all three are overwhelming.

Shortcut 2. I have already stressed that one of the first responsibilities of a committee is to find an expert to rely on. We must rely on a professional investment staff, or else a consultant, or if the fund is too small to afford either of these, then a member of our committee who is a professional in the investment of endowment or pension funds. There are innumerable instances in this book where I refer to our "staff, consultant, or other source of investment expertise." This phrase is entirely too cumbersome, so I have substituted the term *adviser*, and the italics denote that this term stands for our "staff, consultant, or other source of investment expertise."

Shortcut 3. Unless our *fund* manages its investments in-house, which in most case is inadvisable, it needs to hire investment managers or invest in commingled funds such as mutual funds. There are innumerable instances in this book where I refer to our "investment managers or commingled funds such as mutual funds." This phrase also is entirely too cumbersome, so I have substituted the term *investment manager* or simply *manager*, and again the italics denote that this term stands for "investment manager or commingled fund such as a mutual fund."

If the word "manager" is not in italics, then we are referring to the particular person who manages a separate account or commingled fund.

Shortcut 4. Throughout this book, in referring to investment managers, *advisers*, or committee members, I shall for convenience's sake use the masculine pronoun. In all such cases, the "he" is used in the classical sense as a shorthand to designate "he or she." In the current age, this may open me to criticism, and I'm sorry if it does. Clearly, investing is every bit as much a woman's world as a man's world.

CHAPTER 1

The Investment Committee

Who is responsible for the investment of our *investment fund*? Ultimately, the board of directors of the fund's sponsor is responsible. But it is not practical for boards of directors to make investment decisions for the fund, so the board almost always appoints an investment committee to take on this responsibility.

STANDARDS TO MEET

Members of the investment committee are fiduciaries. What does this mean? State laws differ in the precise way they define the term. Many funds look to the federal law for private pension plans—ERISA (the Employees Retirement Income Security Act of 1974)—for guidance, even though the law does not in any way apply to public pension plans or endowment funds. Key standards of ERISA, as adapted for an endowment fund, would be:

1. All decisions should be made solely in the interest of the sponsoring organization.

2. The investment portfolio should be broadly diversified—"by diversifying the investments of the plan so as to minimize the risk of large losses, unless under the circumstances it is clearly prudent not to do so."

3. "The risk level of an investment does not alone make the investment per se prudent or per se imprudent. . . . An investment reasonably designed—as part of the portfolio—to further the purposes of the plan, and that is made upon appropriate consideration of the surrounding facts and circumstances, should not be deemed to be imprudent merely because the investment, standing alone, would have . . . a relatively high degree of risk."[1]

---

[1]Preamble to Final DOL Reg § 2550.404a-1, reprinted in *Preambles to Pension and Benefit Regulations*, 80,352 and 80,354 RIA (1992).

Specifically, the prudence of any investment can be determined only by its place in the portfolio. This was a revolutionary concept, as the old common law held that each individual investment should be prudent of and by itself. There are a great many individual investments in *investment funds* today—such as start-up venture capital—that might not be prudent of and by themselves but, in combination with other portfolio investments, contribute valuable strength to the overall investment program.

4. The standard of prudence is defined as "the care, skill, prudence, and diligence under the circumstances then prevailing that a prudent man acting in a like capacity and familiar with such matters would use in the conduct of an enterprise of a like character and with like aims." This is often referred to as the "prudent expert" rule and strikes me as an appropriate standard. Everyone involved in decision making for the fund should be held to this standard. This does not mean that committee members should be experts. But they should be relying on experts.[2]

That said, I fear that the words "fiduciary" and "prudence" have all too often been impediments to investment performance because of the scary emotional overtones those terms arouse. Such emotions lead to a mentality such as "It's okay to lose money on IBM stock but don't dare lose money on some little known stock." Neither should be more nor less okay than the other.

Prudence should be based on the soundness of the logic and process supporting the hiring and retention of an *investment manager*, and on an a priori basis—not on the basis of Monday morning quarterbacking. According to the Center for Fiduciary Studies, "Fiduciary liability is not determined by investment performance, but rather by whether prudent investment practices were followed."[3]

---

[2]With respect to charitable trusts and charitable corporations, the Uniform Management of Institutional Funds Act issued in 1972 by the National Conference of Commissioners on Uniform State Laws (NCCUSL) includes provisions that are generally consistent with the above standards. For a discussion of that Act and the states that have adopted it, see John Train and Thomas A. Melfe, *Investing and Managing Trusts Under the New Prudent Investor Rule* (Boston: Harvard Business School Press, 1999), pp. 128–131 and 173–182. With respect to personal trusts, see discussion of standards (also generally consistent) promulgated by the American Law Institute in 1992 and the NCCUSL in 1994, ibid., pp. 24–34.

[3]Donald B. Trone, Mark A. Rickloff, J. Richard Lynch, and Andrews T. Rommeyer, *Prudent Investment Practices: A Handbook for Investment Fiduciaries* (Center for Fiduciary Studies, 2004), p. 8.

Another aspect of my concern is that the terms "prudence" and "fiduciary" all too often motivate decision makers to look at what other funds are doing and strive to do likewise on the assumption that this must be the way to go. An underlying theme of this book is that this is not necessarily the way to go. As fiduciaries, we should do our own independent thinking and apply our own good sense of logic.

Everything comes down to facts and logic. Do we have all relevant facts we can reasonably obtain? Are the facts accurate? What are the underlying assumptions? We should ask questions, ad nauseam if necessary. Does a proposal make sense to us? If not, challenge it. And we should work hard to articulate our reasons.

COMMITTEE ORGANIZATION AND FUNCTIONS

Organization

Well, who should be on this all-important fiduciary committee? A committee may consist of outside investment professionals, as is often the case with some of the members of endowment committees of large universities, or the committee may be composed of a group of members of the sponsoring organization (perhaps including certain members of the board of directors), none of whom may have any special expertise in investing. All should meet the criteria listed on page xiv of the Introduction to this book.

What does the fiduciary committee do, and how should it function?

Initially, the committee may adopt a written Operating Policy that addresses such things as committee membership, meeting structure and attendance, and committee communications. As part of this Operating Policy, it should specify the *adviser* on whom the committee will rely, so selecting the *adviser* is the committee's first job. A sample Operating Policy is included at the end of this chapter as Appendix 1.

Then the committee should adopt a written statement of Investment Policies, such as those described in Chapter 3, including the fund's Policy Asset Allocation. These are clearly the committee's most important functions—ones that will have more impact on the fund's future performance than anything else the committee does. After that, the committee must decide whom to hire and retain as *investment managers*. All of these matters are a big responsibility, and the committee will need to rely heavily on its *adviser* for help.

Selecting an *Adviser*

The Uniform Prudent Investor Act empowers fiduciaries to "delegate investment and management functions that a prudent trustee of comparable skills could properly delegate under the circumstances." Jay Yoder, writing for the Association of Governing Boards of Universities and Colleges, adds that "because investing an endowment or any large pool of money is a complex and specialized task requiring full-time professional attention, I would argue that fiduciaries may even be required to delegate responsibilities."[4]

Yoder argues forcefully for a strong investment office: "Endowments of $150 million and larger can and should create an investment office and hire a strong chief investment officer. . . . Hiring a consultant is no substitute for employing a strong investment office." A first-rate internal staff "can be expected to produce a stronger, more advanced investment policy . . . much better implementation of that policy; early adoption of new asset classes and strategies; greater due diligence and monitoring of managers; and, most important, better, more timely decision making."[5]

Many *investment funds* are too small to afford a first-rate internal staff to recommend the asset classes in which they should invest and then select the best *investment managers* in those asset classes. Those funds therefore need to hire an outside consultant who understands the benefits of diversification and who specializes in trying to find the best *managers* in each asset class.

Such a consultant could be our local bank. Some banks have developed expertise in mutual funds, but most would rather guide us into investment programs managed by their own trust departments, very few of which rank among the better investment managers. And few banks have cutting-edge competence in asset allocation.

Many brokers and insurance company representatives offer mutual fund expertise. But can we expect totally unbiased advice from them when they are motivated to gravitate to the range of *investment managers* that compensate them? Many such consultants are paid through front-loaded mutual funds—those that charge an extra 3% to 8% "load" (read "selling commission")—or those that charge an annual 0.25% through a so-called 12(b)(1) deduction from assets (read "another form of selling commis-

---

[4]Jay A. Yoder, *Endowment Management: A Practical Guide* (Association of Governing Boards of Universities and Colleges, 2004), p. 13.
[5]Ibid., pp. 54 and 46.

sion")—or those that charge a back load when we sell the mutual fund, or get compensated in some other way.

A consultant's advice is more likely to be unbiased if the firm's only source of compensation is the fees that it charges its investor clients. Its direct fees will be higher, of course. But we will know fully what the consultant is costing us because none of its compensation will be coming through the back door.

If such a consultant recommends mutual funds to us, he will typically steer us toward no-load mutual funds that do not charge 12(b)(1) fees. Many world-class mutual funds fit this category. On occasion, the consultant might steer us toward a load fund or one with 12(b)(1) fees. If so, the consultant's only motivation should be that he believes future returns of that mutual fund, net of all fees, will still be the best in its particular asset class.

I suggest that an *investment fund*, in hiring a consultant, require the following:

1. The consultant should acknowledge in writing that it is a fiduciary of the pension plan (or the foundation or endowment fund).
2. The consultant should make a written representation *annually* that either:
   a. It receives no income, either directly or indirectly, from investment management firms, or
   b. If it does receive such income, the names of all investment managers from whom it has received such income during the prior 12 months, and in each case, the approximate amount of income and the services provided.
3. The consultant affirms it is prepared to provide to the *fund* all the services included in this book as expected from a *fund's adviser*.

It is easier to draw up the criteria for selecting such a consultant than to find and hire one. Some members of the committee may, in their regular businesses, have contact with investment consultants for whom they have high regard. But we shouldn't necessarily stop there. We can look in consulting directories, such as that provided by the A.S.A.P. Investment Consulting Directory, whose web site lists 74 consultants and whose volume titled *Investment Consultant Directory* lists 380 consultants.

How should we decide among alternative consultants? If we as committee members have first gained some perspective by reading a book such as this one, we will be better prepared to send prospective consultants a questionnaire, to place a consultant's response and presentation in perspective, and to ask meaningful questions.

Our selection should be based on the consultant's track record with other institutional funds, and on the predictive value we feel we can attribute to that track record when we evaluate all the subjective factors—including breadth of diversification in his approach, and continuity of staff.

Role of Committee Members

Once the committee decides on its *adviser*, the committee must expect to approve most of the *adviser's* recommendations. And if the committee has lost confidence in its *adviser*, it must make a change and get an *adviser* in whom it can place its confidence.

Does that mean that once the committee has an *adviser* in whom it has confidence, it should essentially turn all decisions over to him? No, decisions on investment objectives are not readily delegated. They should be developed in the context of the needs and financial circumstances of that particular plan sponsor. Authority to hire and fire *investment managers* may be delegated to an *adviser* who is registered with the SEC as an "investment adviser," but even then the committee has the responsibility to monitor results. The committee's written Operating Policies should specify which actions the *adviser* is authorized to take upon his own judgment, and which actions must first be approved by the committee.

What, then, should we as committee members do? We should ensure that the fund's objectives are consistent with the financial condition of the plan sponsor, and we should ensure that the fund's investment policies are consistent with the plan's objectives. Then we should review each of the *adviser's* recommendations from the following standpoints:

- First and foremost, is the recommendation consistent with the fund's objectives and policies? If not, should the committee consider modifying its objectives and policies, or is the recommendation therefore inappropriate?
- Is the recommendation consistent with the committee's Policy Asset Allocation? If not, should the committee consider modifying its Policy Asset Allocation?
- Is the recommendation internally consistent?

- Has the *adviser* researched all of the right questions relative to things such as:
  - Character and integrity of the recommended *investment manager*,
  - Assessment of the predictive value of the *manager's* track record,
  - Nature of the asset class itself,
  - Credentials of the *manager's* key decision makers,
  - Depth of the *manager's* staff,
  - The *manager's* decision-making processes and internal controls.
- What alternatives did the *adviser* consider?
- Have adequate constraints and controls been established, especially with respect to derivatives that a manager may be authorized to use?
- Does the fee structure seem appropriate?
- Is the recommendation consistent with all applicable law?

Does this sound like a heavy-duty demand on investment sophistication? Although investment sophistication helps, it's not among the criteria for committee members as I've listed them in the Introduction to this book.

Should a committee strive to include at least some investment professionals among its members? In many cases, investment professionals contribute valuable experience to the committee. They can sometimes suggest particular managers for the *adviser* to consider and perhaps open doors that might otherwise be closed.

But investment professionals should be conscious of any conflicts of interest. And if their experience is focused on particular investment areas, they may be less comfortable considering recommendations about other investment areas. Do they understand their limitations? To be successful committee members, they must become generalists, not specialists. Unless they can make this transition, their investment experience can actually be a drawback.

"What is the difference between competent and incompetent boards?" write Ambachtsheer and Ezra in their book *Pension Fund Excellence*.[6] "Competent boards have a preponderance of people of character who are comfortable doing their organizational thinking in multiyear time frames. These people understand ambiguity and uncertainty, and are still prepared

---

[6]Keith P. Ambachtsheer and D. Don Ezra, *Pension Fund Excellence* (New York: John Wiley & Sons, Inc., 1998), p. 90.

to go ahead and make the required judgments and decisions. They know what they don't know. They are prepared to hire a competent CEO[7] and delegate management and operational authority, and are prepared to support a compensation philosophy that ties reward to results."

Committee procedures usually call for decisions to be decided by a majority vote. In practice, it is best if most decisions are arrived at by consensus. That doesn't mean that everyone must agree that a decision is the best possible, but everyone should ultimately agree that it is at least a *good* decision.

Number of Committee Members

How many members should compose the investment committee? This is not a committee that needs to be representative of the different constituencies that may compose the sponsor. This committee has a technical purpose, not an organizational policy purpose.

I favor a smaller committee of members who will take their responsibility seriously and will attend meetings regularly. A committee of five might be optimal for purposes of generating good discussion, giving each member a feeling he is important to the committee, and—not inconsequentially—the ease of assembling the committee for a meeting.

It is for the last reason that I am wary of including out-of-town members on an investment committee. Out-of-town members can bring special qualifications, but they must commit to attending regularly scheduled meetings in person, if possible. They must also be ready to participate in meetings called on relatively short notice to address a special investment opportunity or an unexpected problem. Conference calls, in combination with e-mails and overnight delivery of advance information, can facilitate full participation in such special meetings. Conference calls, however, should ideally be kept to half an hour.

Role of *Adviser*

The *adviser* and his people must be the source of expertise and the ones who do the work. But they should always remember that the investment

---

[7]The pension fund's Chief Executive Officer (or Chief Investment Officer). For example, the staff's director of pension investments. For our purposes, we might substitute the term *adviser*.

committee is the one deciding on the objectives and policies, making the actual investment decisions, and shouldering the final responsibility. The *adviser* cannot be moving in one direction and the committee in another.

This fact leads to what I believe is the number-one responsibility of the *adviser*: to provide continuing education to the committee members. Few committee members start out with a broad grasp of the issues that fill the pages of this book. It is up to the *adviser* to teach them. Such education—including the setting of realistic expectations for return and volatility—should be provided on a continuing basis. Each decision opportunity should be related to the fund's investment policies.

What can the *adviser* do routinely for committee education? The following may be helpful if done regularly, whether times are good or bad:

- Demonstrate the need for a long-term orientation and the futility of short-term thinking.
- Illustrate how the various security indexes have compared with one another at different times over the last 30 years.
- Compare the price/earnings ratio, dividend yield, and earnings-per-share growth rate of today's stock market with their historic norms.
- Show a matrix of future total returns of the stock market as a factor of future P/Es and EPS growth rates.
- Carry out Efficient Frontier studies, using as many asset classes as possible and, if feasible, using Monte Carlo probability methods.
- When analyzing a recommended or existing *investment manager*, show how the *manager* performed relative to his benchmark (or benchmarks) over a variety of different intervals, not just intervals to the latest date.
- If possible, arrange an occasional off-site conference and bring a range of noted investment thinkers—not necessarily the fund's *investment managers*—to discuss in an informal and extemporaneous way the fund's current investment strategy and other questions related to investment philosophy.

Advisers at times have come upon a highly attractive but offbeat investment opportunity but have not considered recommending it to the committee for fear they would be laughed out of the room. To the extent this is true, it is a sorry reflection on the openmindedness of the committee, a reflection on the inadequate education given the committee by the *adviser*, or both. Offbeat opportunities may require much greater due diligence and more careful explanation to committees than more traditional opportunities. But offbeat opportunities, if they pass this test, can add valuable diversification to a fund's overall portfolio.

INTERACTION OF COMMITTEE AND ADVISER

Committee Meetings

We might well set dates a year in advance for meetings—whatever number of meetings may be expected to be necessary. That way, committee members can plan their calendars around those dates. But the committee should be available for interim, unscheduled meetings if needed.

Many organizations simply plan four meetings a year—at the end of each quarter to review results for the quarter. I do not favor that approach. Most such meetings consist mainly of a myopic review of the markets during the last quarter and how each *investment manager* performed. Performance summaries should be sent to committee members in advance—and reviewed by them as part of their expected homework. At meetings, discussion of performance should respond to any question and focus on lessons to be learned or decisions to be made, such as:

- Should we consider terminating one of our current *managers*, or changing his benchmark, or adding money to his account, or withdrawing money from his account?
- Should we be looking for a new *manager* in some asset class?
- Is there a reason why we should consider revising our investment policy or target asset allocation?

It is sufficient for the *adviser* to mail quarterly results to committee members with an explanation that helps to put those results in a longer time frame perspective. Each meeting should be devoted to consideration of a recommendation or continuing education from the *adviser*.

If the *adviser* happens not to have sufficient business to justify a meeting, the *adviser* should suggest that the committee chairman consider canceling the meeting. If a two-hour meeting is scheduled and the *adviser* needs only half an hour of business, the *adviser* should notify committee members as far in advance as possible.

On the other hand, if the committee is in the process, for example, of selecting the *managers* to fill a revised Policy Asset Allocation, then meetings should be scheduled more often until the process is completed—as often as every week or two. Such a process should be completed in a couple of months, at most, not a year or two.

If an urgent matter arises that can't wait for the next scheduled meeting, a special meeting should be called at whatever date most committee members may be available. If the matter is simple and routine enough, the committee chairman can avoid a special meeting by circulating to committee members by e-mail a "consent to action," which is sufficient to authorize action, when agreed to by a majority of the committee.

Committee members should make every effort to attend all meetings, if not in person, then by conference call—which I have found can work very well.

In any case, relative to recommendations, the *adviser* should send committee members copies of his full presentation materials several days before each meeting. Committee members should review these materials with care, so they'll be prepared to ask better questions during discussions at the meeting. The danger is that a committee member may decide how he will vote on the recommendation prior to the meeting. This he should avoid. Advance preparation should lead to questions, not preconceived minds.

I have found it helpful at meetings if the *adviser* reviews each recommendation page by page. This does not mean reading each page out loud. Every committee member should already have read it. Instead, the *adviser* should discuss briefly the meaning—the "so what"—of the page. This tends to elicit more and better discussion and gives greater assurance that no key considerations have been glossed over.

Once each year, the *adviser* should give a thorough review of the overall fund and of each individual *manager*. The *adviser* should explain why each individual *manager* should be retained and why that *manager* remains the best the fund can obtain in his asset class.

Committee Leadership

Successful investment committees require a strong leader who is focused and able to keep discussion on track, and who can bring committee members to final resolution of issues. In planning the agenda, the chairman should schedule the most important items first. If the committee can't adequately resolve all items on the agenda without rushing, the chairman should strongly consider calling a special meeting in, say, two weeks rather than wait possibly a few months until the next scheduled meeting.

Committee members should understand that by not making a decision, they are actually making one, and sometimes that can be costly.

At the end of each meeting, a careful record of all decisions should be prepared and retained in a permanent file, together with a copy of the *adviser's* recommendation for those decisions.

Long-time Morgan Stanley strategist Barton Biggs has suggested that many investment committees make misguided judgments because of the negative dynamics of group interaction. "Groups of highly intelligent people are reaching bad decisions that reflect the easy, prevailing consensus of what has worked recently. . . . Groupthink plagues every committee, and most don't even know it. . . . The more compatible the group, the more its members respect and like each other, the bigger the committee, and the more 'spectators' that attend meetings, the likelier it is to make bad decisions."[8]

Recommendations to the Committee

Jay Yoder, writing for the Association of Governing Boards of Universities and Colleges, contends that "policy implementation . . . should be delegated to a chief investment officer. This senior investment professional should be authorized to take any actions that are consistent with the investment policy, including hiring and firing managers and rebalancing the portfolio."[9]

Still, many investment committees reserve to themselves decisions on hiring and firing managers. In that case, they should lean heavily on their *adviser.*

In making a recommendation to hire an *investment manager*, the *adviser* should be expected to cover concisely the key questions the committee ought to ask about the *manager*. Generally, such a presentation should provide:

- The precise recommendation, including the full name of the *investment manager*, the amount of money to be assigned to its management, and the particular asset class it will manage.

---

[8]Yoder, op. cit., p. 42.
[9]Ibid., p. 49.

- How does the *manager* fit into the portfolio's overall asset allocation and policies? The *adviser* should include information about the asset class itself if the asset class is relatively new to the committee.
- Who is the *manager*? What are the corporate affiliations, date of founding, location of offices, size of staff, and so on?
- How does the *manager* invest? What distinguishes his investment approach from that of other *managers* in his asset class?
- The *manager's* past performance, and why the *adviser* thinks it has predictive value.
- Risks in the *manager's* approach and how to deal with them.
- Who are the key people, and why do we have confidence in them? How deep is the staff, how long have they been with the firm, and what turnover of people has the *manager* experienced?
- Why do we think the *manager* is the best we can get in that asset class?
- Who are the *manager's* other clients, especially for the same kind of program we are recommending? (This consideration is often overemphasized, since it is not the actions—or inactions—of other funds that should determine what we do.)
- What's the fee schedule, and why is it appropriate?

The presentation should cover only the salient points, not try to snow the committee with the whole study nor, in fact, provide any more than a committee member might be expected to absorb. Does the committee really need to know this? The *adviser* should not try to cover his tail by giving an information dump. Of course, the *adviser* should have a rich depth of additional information and background so that he can answer briefly but with authority any reasonable question that might come up.

Meeting with *Investment Managers*

It is customary for many committees to meet the recommended manager of a separate account or commingled fund . . . and sometimes to meet several "finalist" managers one after the other in what I call a beauty contest. The committee can, at best, determine how articulate the manager is. But articulateness has a low correlation with investment capability. In 20 to 30 minutes, a committee's interview can be little more than superficial. Committee members cannot bring the perspective of having met with hundreds of *managers*, as the *adviser* can, nor can they do the kind of homework the *adviser* should have done. Ultimately, the committee's decision comes down, after discussion, to whether the committee has confidence in the *adviser's* recommendation.

I don't even recommend bringing managers to the committee for routine performance reports—for much the same reasons. I have sat through countless manager reports to committees. These reports generally cover the manager's outlook for the economy (which may have little to do with his investment approach), his interpretation of the account's recent performance, and the particular transactions he has made recently. The reports are superficial, usually highly myopic, leaving the committee members with little more than the general feeling that they have "done their fiduciary duty." A cogent, concise report by the *adviser* can do a better job of surfacing issues and placing things in a helpful perspective for education and decision making.

Bringing a manager to meet with the committee can on occasion be a useful part of the committee's education. It can broaden the minds of committee members and help them feel more connected to the investment world about which they are making decisions.

Working with New Committee Members

Whenever a new person is appointed to the committee, the chairman should devote much effort to bringing the newcomer up to speed quickly with the rest of the committee. The new member should immediately be given key documents, such as the fund's objectives and policies, and its Policy Asset Allocation, together with their underlying rationale.

Understanding the "why" of everything is critically important, and the above documents may well need to be supplemented by one-on-one sessions with the *adviser*.

Proxies

An issue at some committee meetings is, if the committee is using separately managed accounts rather than mutual funds, who should vote the proxies for the many common stocks in the portfolio. Certainly, as share owners, we should see that our proxies are voted responsibly.

But who should vote our proxies? I feel strongly that the investment manager who holds a stock in his account should be the one to vote it. He is in the best position to know what vote would most likely promote the value of that stock.

If we invest in mutual funds, the *adviser* is in the best position to vote mutual fund proxies.

SOCIAL INVESTING

A number of endowment fund sponsors—churches and others—overlay their investment objectives with a set of social goals that constrain them from investing in the stocks and bonds of certain kinds of companies.

This practice was most publicized in the 1980s, when many funds avoided securities of companies that did business in South Africa. Other fund sponsors are sensitive to companies that do business in one or more other categories, such as cigarettes, alcoholic beverages, munitions, chemical fertilizers, and so on. Still other funds consciously allocate a small part of their endowment funds to minority-owned enterprises or other companies they view as performing a particular social good.

Overlaying our investment policies with social objectives is one way to "put our money where our mouth is," and as such, is perfectly appropriate—provided the majority of constituents of that fund sponsor agree with the social objectives and with the costs in terms of lower investment returns. Social investing probably does more to enable investing institutions to be consistent with their principles and probably less, from a practical standpoint, to effect social change.

But how can an organization gain the consensus of its constituency as to what industries to avoid? Tobacco companies might be easy. And maybe munitions . . . but should we even avoid companies for whom munitions are only 1% of their business? How about industries that pollute the environment? Which industries are they? Where should we draw the line?

If a fund sponsor is to take a social investing approach, everyone involved must be realistic about the fact that exercising social investing is likely to be costly, for the following reasons:

- Competent investing is difficult enough. Avoiding any set of companies adds to complexity and reduces the *investment manager's* range of opportunities.
- The best investment managers are competitive people and are driven to achieve the best they can. They tend to avoid clients who want them to observe any particular constraints.
- Very few mutual funds observe social investing constraints and become eligible for consideration. Those few mutual funds that do

social investing have—over the long term—achieved performance that is much closer to the bottom of the pack than the top.

- We must consider whether the social objectives of any social investment mutual fund are the same as our social objectives, those of the fund sponsor.
- Without the use of multiple mutual funds, it is difficult to achieve the wide diversification I believe institutional investors should strive for.
- If we are using a separate account rather than a mutual fund, then social investing has an unintended byproduct: Most large companies are so diversified that social-investing limitations eliminate many of them from consideration. Our remaining universe therefore is more heavily weighted toward small stocks, companies we know less about.
- Social investing may also limit us to investments in U.S. companies, because we may be too unfamiliar with specific foreign companies to know whether or not they meet our social investing criteria.
- Members of the fund sponsor must expend a lot of effort to maintain a complete, accurate, and timely list of companies to avoid. Members must be willing to devote the time.

In short, it is unrealistic to expect as good long-term total investment return from a socially invested investment fund as from one that has no such constraints.

Whether or not an endowment fund pursues social investing, I still recommend that the endowment fund use the Imputed Income method for recognizing income (see Chapter 9). But whereas endowment funds with unconstrained investments might use an Imputed Income formula of 5%[10], I would recommend no more than 4%, perhaps less, for an endowment fund limited by social investing constraints.

The sponsor's board should recognize this reduced investment expectation and buy into it explicitly by lowering the Imputed Income formula. And I think the board has a moral obligation to inform the fund sponsor's constituents and make sure they agree.

If everyone agrees, then of course the board should go ahead with its plans for social investing.

Some fund sponsors try to pursue their social objectives through proxy voting. They have at times introduced and supported motions on a com-

---

[10]Of the average market value of the endowment fund over the past five years.

pany's proxy to effect some social or environmental change. I believe such efforts have done more to sensitize companies to the issues than to effect change *directly*—and that has probably been the realistic expectation by the fund sponsors.

The investment downside of this approach is that we can only vote a company's proxy if we are direct owners of its stock, and that constrains us from using mutual funds or other commingled funds, which are such a convenient and effective means of gaining strong investment management and broad diversification.

The issue of social investing does not arise for pension funds, which are required by ERISA to make all decisions "solely in the interest of participants and beneficiaries" of the pension plan. For funds not governed by ERISA, fiduciary responsibilities seem to suggest that social investing be avoided unless there is a compelling mandate from the plan sponsor on specific issues.

IN SHORT

- All who are involved in decisions for an *investment fund* are fiduciaries and are held to a very high standard.
- Decisions are usually made by an investment committee that typically devotes a relatively few hours per year to the fund. The committee must have a competent *adviser* to rely on.

APPENDIX 1
Example of an Investment Committee's Operating Policies

1. The Committee will consist of [number] members, appointed by [whom]. They will serve [staggered] terms of [number] years and may be reappointed for [number] terms.

2. To be eligible for appointment as a Committee member, a person should be familiar with investments—at least to the extent he or she participates in an employer's defined contribution plan or an IRA, or has other investments in stocks or bonds. He or she should also have a broad and open mind with a willingness to learn, be willing and able to attend all meetings of the Committee, and be prepared to review carefully in advance any materials distributed in preparation for meetings.

3. The chairman will be [appointed by whom or elected by a majority vote of the Committee members].

4. The Committee is to hire
   - A Chief Executive Officer (CEO) who will hire staff and manage the entire investment program, subject to the oversight of the Committee, or
   - A consultant who will advise the Committee on investment policy, asset allocation, and the hiring and monitoring of all Investment Managers.

5. The Committee is to meet at least [four times] a year and at any other time either the Committee chairman, CEO, or any two Committee members request a meeting. There may be occasions, in order to complete specific Committee business, when the Committee may have to meet multiple times within a month.

6. Committee members are to make every effort to attend each Committee meeting. If a member cannot attend in person, he or she should participate by conference call.

7. Committee members who participate in fewer than 80% of meetings over a rolling two-year interval are to be terminated from the Committee, subject to a majority vote for retention by the remaining Committee members.

8. Because it is essential to avoid even a perception of conflict of interest, the Committee should consider preparing a Code of Ethics, to be reviewed with legal counsel, which will deal with the appropriate conduct for Committee and staff members. The Code should deal with investment transactions, conflicts of interest, and independence issues, and it should be reviewed and signed by each member of the Committee and staff annually.

9. The Committee will establish statements of Operating Policies and Investment Policies. The latter is to include a Policy Asset Allocation and a related Benchmark Portfolio. Draft policy statements are to be submitted by the CEO [or consultant], who may propose amendments to these statements at any time. Both policies should be reviewed annually.

10. The CEO [or consultant] is to act at all times within the Committee's Operating Policies and Investment Policies. If so authorized, the CEO may deviate from the Committee's Policy Asset Allocation within any range the Committee may establish for an asset class, but he or she is

to report promptly to the Committee any deviation from the Policy Asset Allocation and the reasons for that change.

11. Prior to any Committee meeting, the Committee chairman, upon the recommendation of the CEO [or consultant], will establish the agenda. Wherever possible, the CEO [or consultant] will mail presentation materials to Committee members in time for them to receive the materials a week before the meeting. Committee members are expected to review these materials in preparation for the meeting.

12. The Committee will appoint a secretary, who will prepare minutes of all actions decided by the Committee, and retain these minutes, together with any presentation materials recommending those actions, in a permanent file.

13. Decisions by the Committee are to be made by majority vote, although Committee members should first endeavor to reach a consensus.

14. The Committee, at the recommendation of the CEO [or consultant], will appoint a master custodian, and all fund assets are to be held by the master custodian.

15. The fund may not borrow money except for overnight emergencies, although the Committee may authorize specific Investment Managers of the fund to use leverage.

16. The CEO [or consultant] will submit to Board members a brief quarterly report in writing, including
    - Recent performance (net of fees) versus benchmarks, in the context of the long term;
    - Current asset allocation versus Policy Asset Allocation;
    - Principal actions implemented by the CEO [or consultant] since the last quarterly report;
    - Potential issues or actions for future meetings.

17. The CEO [or consultant] will submit to the Committee a detailed annual report in writing on investment results and follow it with a thorough verbal presentation to the Committee. At this meeting, the CEO [or consultant] will comment on the continued appropriateness of current Operating and Investment Policies and the rationale for continuing to retain each of the fund's Investment Managers.

18. The Committee will select an accredited accounting firm as the fund's auditor, which will submit an annual audit report to the Committee.

19. The fund will publish an annual report, cosigned by the Committee chairman and CEO [if there is one], that will include:
    - Investment results,
    - Year-end asset allocation,
    - Contributions and payouts during the year,
    - Key actions during the year,
    - A summary of the actuarial reports (if for a pension fund),
    - A summary of the audit report,
    - Names of Committee members and key staff members [or consultants],
    - Total compensation paid to or accrued by directors and executive officers,
    - An appendix that includes statements of the Committee's Operating Policy and Investment Policy.

If the Committee employs a CEO and investment staff, rather than relying mainly on a consultant, several more operating policies might be added:

20. Either:
    - The Committee is to approve the selection of all Investment Managers and investment funds; or
    - if the Committee has authorized staff to appoint any Investment Manager or investment fund that is to manage less than [X%] of the fund's assets, any decision involving more than [X%] is to be approved by the Committee. In any case, the Committee must approve the use of any asset class that is being used for the first time.

21. The Committee is to approve any assets to be managed internally—by the CEO and staff.

22. The CEO will have authority to make all decisions that are not reserved for the Committee.

23. Each year, the Committee shall approve an operating budget, submitted by the CEO, covering all fund expenses except fees and expenses of Investment Managers. Fees and expenses of Investment Managers shall not be a part of the budget but shall be summarized in the CEO's annual report to the Committee.

24. The Committee will hire a lawyer, with whom the CEO is to review all legal documents and consult on all legal issues.

Risk, Return, and Correlation

As the investment committee for an *investment fund*, what are we trying to do? We're trying to earn money; more specifically:

- To achieve the highest possible net rate of return over the long term
- While incurring no more risk than is appropriate for the financial circumstances of our fund's sponsor.

Before we go further, we should define what we mean by return and risk, since these are critically important concepts to understand.

RETURN

Whatever game we are learning, whether tennis, bridge, or some other, one of the first things we should learn is how to keep score. How can we know how we are doing if we don't know how to keep score? This is equally true of investing, which I view as a "game" in the classical sense of the term, an extremely serious game.

How do we keep score in investing? The money we earn (or lose) is called "investment return." What constitutes investment return? Investment return on stocks and bonds includes income (such as dividends and interest) and capital gains (or losses), net of all fees and expenses. As basic as that is, we need to keep it in mind. The stock indexes as reported in the newspaper reflect only price—even though dividends have provided investors with close to half of their total return on stocks over the past 75 years. We must add dividends or interest to a stock index to obtain the total return on that index.

Our focus should always be on total return—the sum of income and capital gains (or losses), whether realized or unrealized.[1] Fundamentally, there is little difference between income and capital gains, in that a company or an investor can manipulate the composition of income and capital gains, but one cannot manipulate total return. A company that wants to shield its investors from taxes can pay very low (or no) dividends and reinvest most (or all) of its earnings, either in its business or in the repurchase of its common shares. As investors, we can easily build a portfolio with high or low income, depending on whether we invest in securities that pay high or low dividends and interest. But achieving a high total return remains a difficult challenge.

The final part of the definition of total return is: "net of all fees and expenses." The only return we can count is what we can spend. We must therefore deduct all costs—mainly investment management fees, transaction costs, and custodial expense.

Total return is what investing is all about.

Valuing Our Investments

To find the total return on our investments for any time interval, we must know the value of our investments at the start of the interval and at the end of the interval. But what value? Book value (the price we paid for an investment) or market value?

To understand our investments at any time, we must focus on a single value—market value—the price at which we could most realistically sell those investments at that time. That's what our investments are worth.

Book values are helpful to auditors, and accounting rules require that book values be taken into consideration. (Book values are also extremely important to taxable investors.) But for purposes of understanding our taxfree investments, book values are not helpful.

I often refer to book values as an historical accident. Book value is the price we happened to have paid for our investment on the day we happened to have bought it. A comparison of an investment's market and book values is not enlightening. If the value of our investment is up 50% since we bought it, is that good? If we bought it only a year ago, that's

---

[1]We realize a capital gain (or loss) when we sell a security for a price that is different from what we paid for it. We have an unrealized capital gain (or loss) if the market value of a security we currently own is different from the price we paid for it.

probably good (unless the market rose even more than 50% in that time). But if we bought it 10 years ago, a 50% increase is not very exciting.

Book values also can be manipulated. If we want to show a higher book value for our portfolio, we can sell a security with a large unrealized appreciation (whose price is much higher than its cost), and the book value of our portfolio will rise by the gain we have just realized. Or if we want to show a lower book value, we can sell a security whose price is much lower than its purchase price, and the book value of our portfolio will decline by the loss we have just realized.

Market value cannot be manipulated. Always focus on market values. When making reports about our fund to its board or our sponsor's membership, we should stick with market values. Forget about book values.

What's a Good Rate of Return?

What does it mean when the newspaper says that Mutual Fund X had an annual rate of return of 10% for the past three years? That's simple. It means that if we put a dollar into the mutual fund three years ago, it would have grown by 10% per year. We know that's not 3 times 10 equals 30% for the three years because it's a compound rate of growth. The dollar theoretically became worth $1.10 after Year 1, plus another 10% was $1.21 after Year 2, and another 10% was $1.33 after Year 3. A return of 33% over three years is the same as 10% per year.

Fine. But, is 10% per year good? That depends. Based on the way Mutual Fund X generally invests money, what opportunity did it have to make money? How did the fund's total return compare with that of its benchmark—usually the most appropriate unmanaged index?

Let's say that (a) Mutual Fund X invests mainly in large, well-known U.S. stocks, sticking pretty close to the kinds of stocks included in Standard & Poor's (S&P) 500 index, and that (b) we should expect Mutual Fund X to incur about the same level of risk as the index. In that case, the S&P 500 is a good reflection of the opportunity that the mutual fund faced. The S&P 500 is a sound benchmark. If the total return on the S&P 500 was 13% per year, then the 10% return on Mutual Fund X was not so hot. On the other hand, if the S&P's total return was only 7%, then 10% represents very good performance.

Now wait a moment. Let's turn that around. What if Mutual Fund X returned *minus* 10% per year, and the S&P was off 13% per year. Are we saying that Mutual Fund X performed very well?

Absolutely. Investing in marketable securities is a relative game. We know the market can drop precipitously—and will sometimes. And when it does, Mutual Fund X is just as likely to drop precipitously. We must be aware of that before we buy into Mutual Fund X. As Harry Truman once said, "If you can't stand the heat, get out of the kitchen." If we have selected a valid benchmark for Mutual Fund X, then the most we can ask of Mutual Fund X is to do well relative to that benchmark. I view that as a cardinal rule of investing.

So if the S&P returns 7% and Mutual Fund X returns 10%, then Mutual Fund X is pretty good, right? It's right for that particular year or for whatever interval is being measured. But virtually every mutual fund that has underperformed its benchmark over a long interval can select periods of years when it looked like a hero. And almost every fund with outstanding long-term performance has run into intervals of years when it couldn't meet its benchmark. Hence, evaluating the performance of an *investment manager* on the basis of only one or two intervals, such as the past three or five years, is fraught with danger. What counts is long-term performance, perhaps 10 years or longer.

As board members, we may be asked to decide whether to hire, retain, or terminate a given *investment manager*. Of course we will want to understand historic performance, but what counts is our judgment about the *manager*'s *future* performance. That involves many additional considerations that we will get into in Chapter 6.

In any case, using the right benchmark to evaluate a *manager* is critical. If we have chosen the wrong benchmark, our evaluation might well motivate us to part company with a strong *manager* at the wrong time (or to keep a mediocre *manager*).

So how do we select an appropriate benchmark? Volumes have been written about that. But in essence, a benchmark should represent the particular universe of stocks (or other securities) from which the particular *manager* selects his stocks. We'll talk more about selecting benchmarks for a *manager* in the next few chapters.

Returns on a Portfolio of Investments

We've talked about measuring returns on a single investment. What if we've invested in a whole series of investments? Let's say we invested an increasing amount of money over a period of years, some years more, some years less. In some years, we withdrew some money from our investments. Also, we invested in not one but a portfolio of funds. How do we keep score on a portfolio like that?

There are two basic ways: (1) time-weighted returns, and (2) dollar-weighted returns. It's important to understand the differences between them.

- A time-weighted rate of return measures the rate of return on the first dollar invested during an interval being measured. Every quarter of the year is weighted equally regardless of how much money was in the fund.
- A dollar-weighted rate of return (also called an internal rate of return) measures the rate of return on *every dollar* invested during the interval being measured. For example, a quarter of the year when a lot of new money was invested is weighted proportionately more than a quarter when little money was invested.

We can illustrate the differences most easily with a simple example.

If we put $1,000 into Mutual Fund X and it returns 20% the first year, then at the start of the second year we invest another $5,000 in Mutual Fund Y, and they both return 10% the second year, what is our rate of return on our portfolio of the two funds for the two years?

First, how much money do we have (what is our wealth) at the end of year 2? Our wealth after year 2 is $6,820:

Date	Cash Flow (Contributions and Withdrawals)	Wealth	Investment Return	Rate of Return
1/01/00	$+1,000	$1,000	—	
12/31/00	—	1,200	$200	20%
1/01/01	+5,000	6,200	—	
12/31/01	—	6,820	620	10%

If we weight the results in each year equally (as a mutual fund does), then the annual rate of return for the two years is about the average of 10% and 20%, or roughly 15%.[2] That's the *time-weighted* rate of return—the rate we will be principally concerned with.

---

[2]But be careful of taking simple averages. It's not as simple as it might seem. In this case, the precise annual time-weighted rate of return for the two years is 14.89% $[(1.10 \times 1.20)^{1/2} - 1 = .1489]$

But we did not earn 15% on every dollar. We earned 20% on $1,000, then 10% on a little more than $6,000. What is the *dollar-weighted* annual rate of return on every dollar we had invested? The most accepted way to derive the dollar-weighted rate of return is to calculate the internal rate of return—which turns out to be 11.5%.[3] The 11.5% is what we actually earned on our money. That may be good or bad compared with our long-term aspirations. But it is very difficult to compare that with our opportunities (that is, with any benchmark) to determine whether that is good or bad, because no benchmark would have invested money with the same timing as we have.

Weighting each year equally gives us a figure—15%—that we can compare with other similar funds or with an appropriate benchmark.

Because time-weighted returns ignore the timing of contributions or redemptions, time-weighted returns implicitly relieve the investor of the responsibility for the timing of his investments. That is a critically important assumption. But is it an appropriate assumption?

It depends.

Let's say we placed $1,000 with *Investment Manager* A, and after he achieved a 10% return the first year, we gave him an additional $5,000, and then the stock market dropped 10% and *Manager* A's investment did also. His time-weighted rate of return is about zero (actually –0.5% per year)[4] and his dollar-weighted rate of return is minus 7.4% per year.[5] Shouldn't *Manager* A have known better than to put our money in the stock market just before it went down? If we rely on his time-weighted performance, we're saying no, he should not have known better. But isn't that why we place our money with a professional *investment manager*?

Manager A had an opportunity to be a hero by keeping the money in cash equivalents for the second year, but we are unrealistic if we expect our *manager* to be a good market timer. After more than 30 years of investing, I still don't know of a really good market timer. It is realistic to expect a good *manager* of stocks or bonds to perform well over the long term relative to an appropriate benchmark, but not to be clairvoyant enough to know when to go in or out of the stock market.

Therefore, time-weighted rates of return are best for evaluating a *man-*

---

[3]Note that $6,820 = 1,000(1.1152)^2 + 5,000(1.1152)$.
[4]$(1.10 \times 0.90)^{1/2} - 1 = .995$, or –0.5%.
[5]$1,000 \times 1.10 = 1,100$; $1,100 + 5,000 = 6,100$; $6,100 \times 0.90 = 5,490$, the market value at the end of year 2. Then $5,490 = 1,000(.926)^2 + 5,000(.926)$, and $.926 - 1 = -7.4\%$.

ager of stocks or bonds. They are also the only way to compare the performance of our overall fund with other funds that have had different timing and amounts of cash flows (contributions or withdrawals), or with an overall benchmark for our fund.

But ultimately, time-weighted rates of return are not what count. Dollar-weighted rates of return—also known as internal rates of return—determine our ending wealth. Also, dollar-weighted rates of return are the only meaningful way to measure returns on private investments, where the manager controls the timing of when money goes into and out of the fund.

RISK

Over a 10-year interval, Fund A earned 12% per year while Fund B earned only 10% per year. Both funds had negative returns in some years, but in their negative years Fund A was down 5 percentage points more than Fund B. Which was the better fund?

The answer may depend on our willingness to take on risk. Risk is the flip side of investment return. The higher the expected return, the higher the expected risk. That's a truism—and pretty true (although not always). It doesn't necessarily work the other way, however. The higher the risk does not necessarily mean the higher the return. Casinos, for example, can be high risk, but for the gambler they all have a negative expected return.

What is risk?

Most fundamentally, risk is the probability of losing money—or that the value of our investment will go down. Most investments other than U.S. Treasury bills and insured bank accounts have some reasonable probability of losing money. Other risks are outlined on the following page.

Volatility

The most widely used definition of risk is volatility—how much market values go up and down over time. Volatility is most widely used because it is the most measurable of all risks. Also, over long intervals of time, the volatility of a portfolio encompasses most of the above risks. Volatility measures the uncertainty surrounding an investment, or a portfolio of investments. Because it is measurable, it is more controllable.

How do we measure volatility? The simplest measure is annual standard deviation from the asset's (or portfolio's) mean rate of return, the same standard deviation measure we may have learned to calculate in high

EXAMPLES OF SPECIFIC RISKS

- **Loss of Buying Power.** We could go many years without losing money and yet have suffered very real risk. A passbook savings account, for example, would not have lost money, but its buying power at the end of a long interval would be lower than when it started if its rate of return failed to keep up with inflation.

- **Theft.** The risk of dealing with someone, perhaps several times removed from the person we're dealing with, who turns out to be a thief. Some mighty sophisticated investors have at times put large amounts of money into a company only to find out that the inventory the auditor signed off on simply wasn't there, and the company was heading for bankruptcy. There are countless ways for dishonest people to separate us from our money. We can't afford to compromise on the character and trustworthiness of the people with whom we do business. Trust is a sine qua non.

- **Complexity.** Many a person has gotten into investments too complex for him to understand. The press has reported numerous disasters involving derivatives, some of which can have complexities that are very difficult for mere mortals to fathom.

- **Loss of Control.** A portfolio of investments can become so large and diverse that it gets beyond our ability to understand or beyond what we (or our organization) are prepared to manage.

- **Illiquidity.** When we have our money tied up in some nonmarketable investment, we may suddenly need to use the money or would like to sell the investment, and can't.

- **Maverick Risk.** Making investments that none of our peers is making. Because the investments are offbeat, we might fear being viewed as imprudent for straying from the pack if one of the investments goes sour.

- **Benchmark Risk.** Varying too much from a benchmark. If an *investment manager's* returns have too much variance from his benchmark, how do we know whether or not he is doing a good job? If our overall portfolio strategy strays too far from its benchmark, are we still really in control?

EXAMPLES OF SPECIFIC RISKS *(Continued)*

■ **Putting Too Many Eggs in One Basket.** No matter how confident we are about an investment, there is always some possibility that it will go sour. The flip side is that many of the wealthiest people did just that—focused most of their wealth and energies on a single investment that proved very successful. But we don't hear about the large number who followed the same approach, then went down the tubes. Bankruptcy courts are full of them.

school or college algebra. A low standard deviation of investment returns over time means we had pretty high certainty of investment results. A high standard deviation means we had a high degree of uncertainty. Low volatility is good, high is bad.

The term "standard deviation" can be pictured in the context of a curve of probabilities, as in Figure 2.1. The higher the standard deviation, the wider the curve. The lower the standard deviation, the narrower the curve.

Standard deviation works well in computer models that help us decide the Policy Asset Allocation of our fund—how much of our fund should be

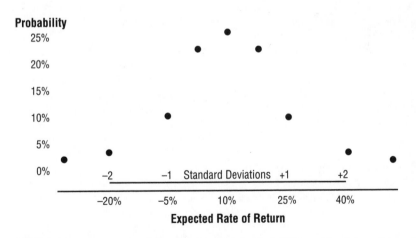

FIGURE 2.1 Bell Curve of Expected Return Probabilities, with a Mean Expected Return of 10% and a Standard Deviation of 15%

allocated to various kinds of stocks and bonds, for example. (That decision is the most important decision our committee will have to make. We'll discuss that in Chapter 4.)[6]

Systematic Risk and Diversifiable Risk

Most individual U.S. stocks bounce up and down more than the overall U.S. stock market. We can ease that roller-coaster ride—reduce that volatility—by adding more U.S. stocks, especially ones in different industries that march to a somewhat different drummer. We can strive to eliminate this diversifiable risk. But after a point, we will still be left with the "systematic risk" of the overall U.S. stock market.

Through statistical methods known as regressions, we can divide the volatility of each U.S. stock into portions that are:

1. Systematic with the overall U.S. stock market.
2. Systematic with its own industry.
3. Systematic with stocks that have similar price/earnings ratios.
4. Systematic with stocks that have certain other common characteristics.
5. Not systematic with any of those characteristics. This is residual risk.

---

[6]There are multiple ways to calculate annual volatility, and different ways can give different results (as by annualizing daily or quarterly volatility). Moreover, standard deviations assume that every investment has a normal bell curve distribution of returns. Some investments, however, have highly skewed distributions of returns. In short, standard deviations have a lot of fuzz around them. But they may be the best measure we have.

Other measures of risk are semivariance, shortfall risk, and betas. We needn't worry about them, but let's define betas in case we hear the term used. Betas compare the price movements of any stock (or portfolio) with those of the overall stock market (commonly but not necessarily measured by the S&P 500). Does Stock A go up more than the market when the market goes up, and down more than the market when the market does down? Or does Stock A tend to move less than the market? Beta is an effort to provide that measure.

A beta of 1.0 means that Stock A has tended to move up and down with the market. A beta of 1.2 means that when the market was up 10%, Stock A tended to be up 1.2 times 10%, which is 12%, and when the market was down 10%, Stock A tended to be down 12%. (Conversely, a beta of 0.8 means that, when the market moved 10%, Stock A tended to be up or down only 8%). Beta is part of a regression equation that relates the historical performance of a stock (or of a portfolio of stocks) to the market.

We can diversify away these risks by adding more and different kinds of U.S. stocks. But we can't diversify away volatility that is systematic with the U.S. stock market simply by adding more U.S. stocks. We can reduce this volatility only by adding other assets—non–U.S. stocks, bonds, real estate—assets whose volatility has a relatively low correlation with that of U.S. stocks; the lower the correlation the better.

Diversifiable risk is a critically important concept that we can put to great advantage, as we shall see later in this book.

What To Do About Risk

All of the risks we've mentioned are important. We must understand them all and treat them with due respect. But we must place each into proper perspective and not allow ourselves to become traumatized by risk. If we have a good understanding of the risks, then we should be looking for ways to use risk to our advantage.

We began this chapter with a truism: the higher the expected return, the higher the expected risk. The job of running an investment fund is not to see how little risk we can take, but to see how much risk we can take—diversifiable risk, of course. That is, intelligent diversifiable risk.

This has powerful implications for an investment portfolio. The average individual stock in a large portfolio of stocks might have an annual volatility of 30 percentage points per year, while the volatility of the overall stock portfolio might be closer to 15. We can reduce risk most productively by investing in multiple asset classes that have a low correlation with one another—domestic stocks, foreign stocks, real estate, bonds. What is correlation?

CORRELATION

"Correlation" is a term of investment jargon whose great importance is often underappreciated. Correlation compares the historical relationship of the returns of Stock A (or Portfolio A) with those of a market index or of any other asset with which we want a comparison. Do returns on the two move together? Or do they march to different drummers?

A correlation of 1.0 between Stocks A and B means they have always moved exactly together. A correlation of –1.0 means they have always moved exactly opposite to one another. A correlation of 0 means there has been no relationship whatsoever between the returns of Stocks A and B.

The concept of correlation is the foundation for the concept of systematic risk and diversifiable risk. By assembling a portfolio of assets whose volatilities have a low correlation with one another, we can have a portfolio of relatively risky assets that has a materially higher expected return, but no more volatility than a portfolio of much less risky assets.

RISK-ADJUSTED RETURNS

The Sharpe Ratio

We have now talked extensively about investment return and risk. There are multiple ways to bring them together as "risk-adjusted returns." Perhaps the best-known way is the Sharpe Ratio, named for Dr. William F. Sharpe, a Nobel Prize winner, who devised it. It's not crucial that we understand the Sharpe Ratio, but if we hear it referred to, here's what it is.

Conceptually, the Sharpe Ratio is a simple measure—excess return per unit of risk. Specifically, it's an investment's rate of return in excess of the riskfree (Treasury-bill[7]) rate, divided by the investment's standard deviation. The Sharpe Ratio answers the question: How much incremental return do we get for the volatility we take on?

We can apply this ratio to a single investment or to an entire portfolio. The higher the Sharpe Ratio, the more efficient an investment it is. That does not necessarily mean that if Investment A has a higher Sharpe Ratio than Investment B, then A is always a preferable addition to our portfolio than B. The correlations of A and B with everything else in our portfolio are also very important. Because of the benefit of diversification, our overall portfolio would almost always have a materially higher Sharpe Ratio than the weighted average Sharpe Ratio of our individual investment programs.

---

[7]A Treasury bill, known as a "T-bill," is a very short-term loan to the U.S. government, which is considered to have zero risk.

Conceptually, the Sharpe Ratio "leverages" or "de-leverages" actual returns by saying, in effect: What would be the return if we added T-bills to a volatile investment (de-leveraging the investment) until we have reduced its annual standard deviation to our target volatility? Or what would be the return on a low-volatility investment if we borrowed at T-bill interest rates (leveraging the investment) until we have increased its annual standard deviation to that of our target volatility?

That's a tough concept. Let's tackle it with a simplistic example. Let's say, with T-bill rates at 6%, we have two investments, A and B, with the following characteristics:

	Return	Volatility	Sharpe Ratio	Calculation
A	12%	15%	.4	$(12 - 6)/15 = .4$
B	9	5	.6	$(9 - 6)/ 5 = .6$

B has a higher Sharpe ratio, .6 to .4. That's preferable. But why should we prefer B when the return on A is 3 points higher? Implicitly, if we wanted to get the volatility of B up to the same 15% volatility of A, we would have to leverage—buy three times as much B and borrow two-thirds of the money. The return on our money would be 15%, or 3% more than that of A.

Risk-adjusted returns are viewed by many as the true measure of an *investment manager*. In the sense that less volatility is almost always better than more, it is intuitively appealing to reward the lower-volatility manager appropriately.

Personally, I have not placed a great deal of value on risk-adjusted returns, for two basic reasons:

- We can't spend risk-adjusted returns—only actual returns.
- Our critical measure is not the absolute volatility of a single investment (or a single asset class) but the impact of that investment (or asset class) on the volatility of our overall portfolio. Its impact depends on (a) the correlation of that investment (or asset class) with our other assets and (b) the percentage of our overall portfolio we devote to that investment (or asset class).

Those two basic reasons lead to four corollary reasons:

1. Risk-adjusted returns tend to be theoretical and not real-world, in the sense that, because of unrelated business income tax (UBIT) and other reasons, it is often not feasible to borrow in order to leverage up a low-volatility portfolio. Likewise, we would almost never choose to offset a high-volatility *manager* by adding cash equivalents.

2. While we can afford to have only so many high-volatility *managers* in our portfolio, the most productive way to deal with a high-volatility high-return *manager* is to find another high-return *manager* in another asset class who has a low correlation with him.

3. While the inclusion of a low-volatility *manager* in our portfolio does make room for the inclusion of a high-volatility *manager*, we can gain the proper benefit from that low-volatility *manager* only if we do indeed hire a high-volatility, high-return manager.

4. Of course, we should make sure the high-volatility high-return *manager* doesn't push us beyond the volatility constraint for our overall portfolio. But many endowment funds don't take on as much volatility as they should. We don't deserve accolades for reducing overall portfolio volatility below our target at the cost of lowering our overall portfolio return.

Perhaps the best argument against reducing portfolio risk in traditional ways is one articulated by Keith Ambachtsheer and Don Ezra, who have said we should "consider the opportunity cost of undertaking risk in a different, perhaps more rewarding way."[8]

DERIVATIVES—A BOON OR A DIFFERENT FOUR-LETTER WORD?

Derivatives are so often associated with risk in many people's minds that we should deal with them here. Common examples of derivatives are shown in the box on the following page. Derivative securities are extremely

---

[8]Keith P. Ambachtsheer and D. Don Ezra, *Pension Fund Excellence*, (New York: John Wiley & Sons, Inc., 1998), p. 54.

EXAMPLES OF DERIVATIVES

- **Futures.** Agreements, usually exchange-traded, to pay or receive, until some future date, the change in price of a particular security or index (such as: S&P 500 index futures[9]).

- **Forwards (forward contracts).** Agreements between two parties to buy (or sell) a security at some future date at a price agreed upon today (such as foreign exchange forwards).

- **Swaps.** Agreements between two parties to pay or receive, until some future date, the difference in return between our portfolio (or an index) and a counterparty's portfolio (or an index). For example: "We'll pay you the T-bill rate plus 50 basis points,[10] and you pay us the total return on the *Financial Times* index on U.K. stocks.

- **Call options.** The holder of a call option has the right (but not the obligation) to buy a particular security from the seller of the call option at a particular price by a particular date. The holder can "call" the shares from the option seller. For example, a call option to buy S&P 500 index futures at an index of 1300 by September 15.

- **Put options.** The holder of a put option has the right (but not the obligation) to sell a particular security to the seller of the put option at a particular price by a particular date. The holder can "put" the shares to the option seller. For example, a put option to sell S&P 500 index futures at an index of 1200 by September 15. Options are often traded on a stock or commodity exchange.

- **Structured notes.** Agreements between two parties, the nature of which is limited only by the creative imagination of investment bankers.

---

[9]An S&P 500 index future is an agreement to pay or receive, until some future date, the change in the S&P 500 index. Cash equivalents equal in value to the money we want to invest in the stock markets plus S&P futures would then behave almost exactly like an S&P 500 index fund. An S&P 500 index fund is a portfolio invested exactly like the S&P 500 index.

[10]A basis point equals 0.01%.

valuable tools in managing a portfolio. They enable us to *reduce* risk by hedging out risks we don't want. Through futures, forwards, or options, we can choose to reduce our currency risk, or interest-rate risk, or stock-market risk.

They also can allow us to take more risk if we like.

They can also be big cost savers. For example, if we want to invest in an S&P 500 index fund, the purchase of S&P 500 index futures to overlay a portfolio of cash equivalents may be cheaper (and at least as effective) compared with buying all 500 stocks for our own account. Buying the stocks would entail transaction costs, custodial costs, dividend reinvestment costs, and proxy-voting costs. When it's time to sell, futures are far less cumbersome and costly to sell.

As Nobel laureate Merton Miller has said, "Index futures have been so successful because they are so cheap and efficient a way for institutional investors to adjust their portfolio proportions. As compared to adjusting the proportions by buying or selling the stocks one by one and buying or selling T-bills, it is cheaper to use futures by a factor of 10."[10]

So why all the fuss about derivatives?

First of all, derivatives can be complex, particularly specially tailored derivatives that are not exchange-traded. Many people have purchased derivatives without fully understanding all the specific risks involved and have gotten burned badly.

Other investors, through derivatives, have quietly altered their fund's risk/return position substantially without letting their constituents know until suddenly a blowup has occurred. Recent changes in accounting rules have helped to lessen this risk through a requirement of sunlight—public reporting.

The sheer complexity of certain derivatives—such as those involving options, whose pattern of returns is highly asymmetric—might at times make it difficult for some plan sponsors to assess very accurately their full exposure to the various markets.

---

[10]*Journal of Applied Corporate Finance.*

A 1994 article in Moody's did a good job of summarizing the situation:

> *The financial roadside is littered with the wreckage of poorly run derivatives operations. . . . Even entities with excellent internal controls are not immune from such surprises. . . . Because risk positions can be radically changed in a matter of seconds, derivatives activity has increased the potential for surprise. . . .*
>
> *[But] derivatives often get a bad rap. A frequent message we hear is that anyone who is involved in derivatives transactions is tempting fate, and that sooner or later major losses will be suffered as derivatives positions inevitably go wrong. Such messages are misleading.*
>
> *Properly used, derivatives have been and will continue to be a source of risk reduction and enhanced investment performance for many participants. Therefore, any manager who is not looking at how derivatives can be employed to manage financial and economic risks, or to enhance yields, is doing his or her investors a disservice.*

As committee members, do we have to understand all this about derivatives? No, we don't. Our *adviser* should understand it. But our *adviser* should tell us if a *manager* uses derivatives, and he should explain in words satisfactory to us:

- What derivatives the *manager* uses and why;
- Losses that could result from use of those derivatives in a volatile, illiquid market; and
- The manager's approach to risk control.

Although asset classes that use derivatives (such as some arbitrage programs) require more investor skill to enter, those asset classes are well worth considering by *investment funds*. Where an investor can find competent *managers* and reasonable terms, use of these asset classes can reduce the aggregate volatility of an overall portfolio and also increase its overall expected return. But it pays to be thoughtful about our exposure and to ask good questions.

IN SHORT

- All rates of return should be based on market values. What counts is *total return*, the sum of dividends, interest, and changes in market value (capital gains or losses).
- There are many kinds of risk. Over long intervals there is one measure that encompasses most of them. That's volatility—how much market values go up and down over time.
- We need to be fully aware of the risks in our portfolio, but we should not be traumatized by them. The challenge is to mitigate risks by diversifying our portfolio among assets whose returns are not highly correlated with one another.

CHAPTER 3

Setting Investment Policies

Once we have an *adviser*, our first task as an investment committee is to set down in writing our investment policies. Our policy statement should include our investment objectives, how we will go about investing, and how we will keep score. We should articulate our principles in a way that will serve as criteria against which to evaluate both current investment actions and future proposals.

Well, what is the purpose of any *investment fund*? For an endowment fund or a foundation, it's to provide a reliable and hopefully increasing income to the fund's sponsor. For a pension fund, it's to earn money to pay pension benefits. In either case, we should be striving for the highest long-term rate of return that we can achieve—within whatever risk limits we believe are appropriate, of course.

I should emphasize: This is a long-term game. Good returns over short-term intervals aren't very important except as they contribute to the long-term rate of return. It's the long-term annual rate of return that really counts.

At the end of every game, it's easy to figure out how we've done—what our long-term rate of return was. But no one gets the benefit of 20/20 hindsight when strategizing how to play the game. The only thing that counts is tomorrow, and tomorrow is an unknown—anything can happen. So how do we go about deciding how to invest our money today?

To establish our investment objectives, we must begin by deciding on three interrelated elements as they apply to us:

- Return,
- Risk, and
- Time Horizon.

But these are backward. First, we should decide our time horizon—the number of years until we need to use our money. That determines how much risk we can take with our investments. If we need our money tomorrow, we can't afford any risk. Such money shouldn't be in an endowment fund.

TIME HORIZON, RISK, AND RETURN

Time Horizon

There are major reasons why investing money for an *investment fund* is dramatically different from investing one's personal assets—other than the fact that such institutional funds are taxfree. Endowment funds, for example, have a perpetual life, while most of the payouts by typical pension funds are well more than 10 years out.

If I am investing for my family, I must invest essentially for my spouse, myself, and our children. I really don't know when I will need my savings, and how much I will need, so I must invest conservatively, to prepare for the worst.

An *investment fund* usually knows about what these future payments must be, and the *investment fund* should make the most of this critical advantage. An *investment fund* should therefore invest with a very long time horizon, focusing on rates of return over intervals of 10 or 20 years. Why is this an advantage? Notice from Figure 3.1 how the uncertainty of returns narrows with time like a funnel. Figure 3.1 depicts annual rates of return since 1926 on large U.S. stocks for intervals ranging from 1 to 20 years. It shows that one-year returns on common stock have been almost totally unpredictable. Two-thirds of the time, one-year returns have ranged between +35% and negative 9%. But for 10-year intervals, this span of annual returns has narrowed to a range of +18% to +4%, and the range has narrowed further for longer intervals.

Clearly, an *investment fund* should go for the benefits of being very long-term oriented. But too much volatility will make annual payments to the sponsor too unreliable. This leads to the second element in an investment objective—risk.

Risk

Risk is a hard thing to deal with in setting the investment objectives of a fund. To quantify our sponsor's risk tolerance, our investment committee

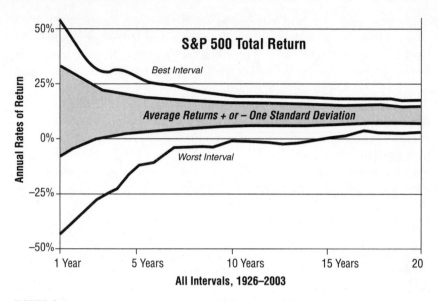

FIGURE 3.1 S&P 500 Total Return for All Intervals, 1926–2003
Source of Data: Ibbotson Associates, *2004 Yearbook*, Chicago, 2004.

could establish the maximum standard deviation of annual returns that we are willing to incur. But that's tough to specify.

The lower the volatility we can withstand, the lower the long-term rate of return we can rationally aspire to achieve, and vice versa. But what does it mean to say, "We would be willing to incur a standard deviation of X percentage points"? If the financial markets are very placid, we'll have no trouble staying within a standard deviation of X percentage points. But if the markets are turbulent, a standard deviation of X percentage points will be a pipe dream. We have no control over future financial markets.

Hence, about the only risk measure that's pragmatic is a *relative* risk measure. For example, we could say, "We can withstand the volatility of the U.S. stock market as measured by the S&P 500, but not higher." Historically, the annual standard deviation of the S&P 500 has been about 17 percentage points. What we must wrestle with is this question: Can we stand the downside volatility of the S&P 500 when it is two or three standard deviations worse than "normal"?

More concretely, could we stand a 1973–1974 or 2000–2002 decline, when an S&P 500 index fund would have lost nearly 40% of its value? Or might our committee lose its nerve at the bottom, decide it should never have been in such a risky investment program, and sell out at precisely the wrong time? At the end of 1974 or 2002, such a change of direction would have been a disaster, as the market regained in the next two years all it had lost in 1973–1974 and was up sharply in 2003–2004.

That's the kind of question we should ask ourselves. Conceptually, an *investment fund* should be able to withstand that level of volatility, but from a pragmatic standpoint, can our sponsor's board of directors, or its future board, withstand it?

That is why, as a benchmark for our total fund, we might establish a hypothetical portfolio of index funds—a "Benchmark Portfolio." Our objective would be to incur volatility not greater than that of our Benchmark Portfolio.

How could we know whether a particular Benchmark Portfolio was appropriate for us? We might see what the volatility of the Benchmark Portfolio would have been over various long intervals of years and see whether we, our committee, and our sponsoring organization could stand that level of volatility.

I think many institutions set their volatility constraint too low relative to the time horizon that they should establish. As Jack Bogle, founder of the well-known Vanguard Group, has said, "One point of added volatility is meaningless, while one point of added return is priceless."

Return

Our return objective is simple. We want the highest long-term rate of return we can achieve without exceeding our risk constraint.

POLICY ASSET ALLOCATION

Benchmark Portfolio

Well, where does our Benchmark Portfolio come from? It is a way to measure the index returns on our Policy Asset Allocation, which we must decide on first. Our Policy Asset Allocation defines the percentage of our portfolio that we shall target for each asset class. In the next chapter, we shall talk more about how we might go about deciding on our Policy Asset Allocation.

The Benchmark Portfolio, by measuring the volatility of our Policy Asset Allocation, quantifies the maximum risk we are willing to incur. Does it also define our return objective as well?

One of the good things about a Benchmark Portfolio is that it sets a relative objective, not an absolute objective. An absolute objective would be something like, "We want to earn 10% per year." Over an extremely long term, like 20 or 30 years, an absolute objective—especially in real terms (net of inflation)—might be an appropriate objective. For intervals of fewer years, however, relative objectives are more appropriate, because we are all prisoners of the market.

But using the return on our Benchmark Portfolio as our investment return objective still seems inadequate. I think a more appropriate objective would be "to earn the highest possible rate of return without incurring more risk than the risk of our Benchmark Portfolio." We should be greedy, aim for the best possible return—as long as we stay within our risk constraint (set by our Benchmark Portfolio).

We can achieve a rate of return equal to our Benchmark Portfolio if we invest in index funds identical to that Portfolio. Therefore index returns on our Benchmark Portfolio should be the minimum return we should aspire to earn long-term.

We suggested earlier that diversification can help us get more bang for each point of our portfolio's volatility. We should therefore build this diversification into our Policy Asset Allocation and Benchmark Portfolio. We should include any asset class we believe will improve our portfolio's aggregate return without increasing its aggregate volatility beyond the limit we believe is acceptable.

We should review our Policy Asset Allocation periodically for appropriateness, but we should change it only with compelling reason. Theoretically, of course, the best results would come from reducing our allocation to stocks before stocks enter a bear market and increasing the allocation before stocks enter a bull market. There are few if any professional investors who have been able to do this successfully over time, and probably most would have been better off if they hadn't tried.[1]

Therefore, let's not try to time the market. Let's try to maintain our Policy Asset Allocation over the long term. Our Policy Asset Allocation—and our Benchmark Portfolio, which measures that allocation—should be quite stable over time.

---

[1]Fidelity Management Company has placed market timing in good perspective with its "Louie the Loser" illustration. Louie invested consistently the same amount of money every year for 20 years, 1978–1997—but unfortunately, always when the market hit its high for the year. He still had a compound annual return over the 20 years of 15.7%. By comparison, if he had invested each year when the market had hit its low for the year, his compound annual return would have been only 1.5 points higher—17.2%.

BENCHMARKS FOR MARKETABLE SECURITIES

For each asset class of marketable securities, we should use an index as its benchmark. After all, if we have no rational expectation to exceed the index return of an asset class, we should invest in an index fund for that asset class.

The traditional index used as a benchmark for U.S. stocks is the S&P 500. This is not an adequate benchmark for our U.S. stocks. The S&P 500 is essentially a large-stock index with a growth-stock bias. Even though it measures about 81% of the market capitalization of all stocks traded in the U.S., our feet should be held to the fire of all marketable stocks in the U.S.

Perhaps the best measure of all U.S. stocks is the Russell 3000 index. The Russell 3000, like the S&P 500, is a capitalization-weighted index,[2] but it consists of the 3,000 largest stocks in the United States and measures more than 98% of the market capitalization of all U.S. stocks. It is preferable, in my opinion, to treat large and small U.S. stocks as two separate asset classes, using the Russell 1000 for large and the Russell 2000 for small.[3]

But U.S. stocks account for only about half the capitalization of all marketable stocks in the world. Therefore, for the purpose of diversification, we should include non-U.S. stocks separately in our Benchmark Portfolio.

The most widely used index of non-U.S. stocks is the Morgan Stanley Capital International (MSCI) index for Europe, Australia, and the Far East (EAFE). This also is an inadequate benchmark for our portfolio. It fails to include Canadian stocks, smaller stocks, or those of the emerging markets—Latin America, much of Asia, eastern Europe, and Africa. A better benchmark is the MSCI All Country Index, ex. U.S. Or, better yet, I suggest treating emerging markets stocks as a separate asset class, in which case we might use the MSCI World Index, ex. U.S. to cover common stocks of the developed markets and then use the MSCI Emerging Markets Free Index for the emerging makets.

For fixed income, the broadest index of investment-grade U.S. bonds has long been the Lehman Aggregate Bond Index.

BENCHMARKS FOR MARKETABLE SECURITIES *(Continued)*

As an investment committee member, am I expected to know about the various indexes that might be used as benchmarks? No, but a little knowledge about the main indexes will allow us to ask useful questions of our *adviser*.

Once we establish our Benchmark Portfolio, we can see how the performance of our portfolio compares. If, over intervals of three to five years our performance does not at least equal that of our Benchmark Portfolio, we should be asking hard questions as to why.

---

[2]A cap-weighted index weights each stock in direct proportion to its capitalization—its number of shares outstanding (or available for trading) times the price of its stock. Almost all stock indexes are *cap-weighted*. That is, a stock like GE, which may have a cap of $300 billion, is weighted 3,000 times as heavily as a micro-cap stock with a capitalization of only $100 million. There is an elegance to cap-weighted indexes:

- They reflect the total market value of all stocks in the index.
- We can create a portfolio that contains the same stocks in the same proportions as the index (an index fund), and if properly assembled the portfolio's performance should very precisely mirror that of the index. We'll talk more about index funds in Chapter 6 in the context of selecting investment managers.
- Cap-weighting is appropriate because all investors together *must* hold the same aggregate value in each stock as its capitalization, and they can hold no more aggregate value in each small stock than its capitalization. Although any individual investor can be different, all investors together cannot.

We haven't even mentioned the best-known stock index of all—the Dow Jones Index of 30 Industrial Stocks. Why not? After all, it's the market barometer most often referred to in the press. The Dow is not a cap-weighted index. Each stock is weighted by a factor relating to its price, unrelated to how many shares are outstanding. It is difficult to manage an index fund of the Dow Jones Industrials. For this reason, while the Dow serves well as a rough measure of the performance of very large U.S. stocks, it is not a very useful analytical tool.

[3]The Russell 1000 includes the 1,000 largest U.S. stocks, and the Russell 2000 the 2,000 next largest.

Selecting the Benchmarks

Well, given a Policy Asset Allocation composed of a range of different asset classes, how do we go about selecting the index that will serve as our benchmark for each asset class? The boxes on the two previous pages suggest the kind of benchmarks that would be appropriate for the most common marketable securities.

Many *investment funds* finesse their investment objectives by using as a benchmark whatever rate of return is earned by their peers, with a target standard deviation of annual investment returns no higher than the average of their peers. I understand the motivations for this, because most institutions are always looking over their shoulder to see if they are doing as well as their peers. But I think this is not an advisable investment objective.

Framing our objectives as a function of what our peers are doing makes us a prisoner of their investment objectives and constraints, whether or not their objectives and constraints are optimal for us. Factors that influence their investment policies may be quite different from those that should influence ours. We should set our investment objectives based on our own independent thinking about the reasons for each part of those objectives. That's because our peers are not always right, especially for our situation. Moreover, they are often influenced by conventional wisdom.

To illustrate differences in conventional wisdom, U.K. pension funds historically invested 80% or more of their portfolios in common stocks, U.S. pension funds 60% to 70%, Canadian pension funds were at one time more like 40%, and Swiss pension funds closer to zero. (Many Swiss pension plans preferred simply to buy annuities.) Such asset allocations are influenced partly by local laws, but in most cases, Company A follows an approach because it's conventional wisdom—it's the approach followed by peers in its country. Aren't all pension funds worldwide trying to do the same thing? An optimal approach for investing a pension fund in one country is probably pretty close to an optimal approach in another country. Except for conventional wisdom—herd mentality.

One who has done his own independent thinking is David Swensen, who has led the Yale University endowment fund to achieve one of the best long-term results among all institutional funds. Swensen "pioneered the move away from heavy reliance on domestic marketable securities, emphasizing instead a collection of asset classes expected to provide equity-like returns driven by fundamentally different underlying factors. Aside from reducing dependence on the common factor of U.S. corporate profitability, the asset allocation changes ultimately exposed the portfolio to a range of less efficiently priced investment alternatives, creating a rich set of active management opportunities."[4]

Hence . . . let's do our own independent thinking, set our own investment objectives.

PREPARING A STATEMENT OF INVESTMENT POLICIES

Ultimately, every *investment fund* should prepare a written statement of investment policies. The following is an example of such a statement.

Investment Policies of XYZ Fund

Overall Objectives. Investment policies and individual decisions are to be made for the exclusive benefit of the endowment fund's sponsor [or for the Pension Plan's participants], and any perception of conflict of interest is to be avoided. Within the relevant laws, investment objectives are:

- **Payments.** Without fail, to make every scheduled payment to the fund sponsor [or to Plan participants] on the date it is due.
- **Liquidity.** To maintain enough liquid assets and other assured sources of cash to cover projected payouts for at least the next five years.

Policy Asset Allocation/Benchmark Portfolio. The Fund's Policy Asset Allocation also serves as its Benchmark Portfolio, with each liquid asset class to be benchmarked against a specified index. Over intervals of five years or longer, the portfolio's net total return is intended to exceed that of the Benchmark Portfolio by as much as possible without the portfolio's overall volatility materially exceeding that of the Benchmark Portfolio.

Quarterly returns on the Benchmark Portfolio are to be calculated as follows:

a. The actual return on illiquid investments (targeted at __% of the portfolio) times their actual percentage of the portfolio at the start of the quarter.

---

[4]David F. Swensen, *Pioneering Portfolio Management* (The Free Press, 2000), p. 1.

b. Index returns on liquid assets (the balance of the portfolio) weighted as shown in Table 3.1.

The Fund should periodically review its Policy Asset Allocation to ensure that it remains appropriate for the needs of the Fund, although it is not expected that changes will need to be made frequently.

Because short-term fixed income securities are the lowest-return asset class over any long-term interval, the Fund should target its holdings of these securities at the lowest possible level commensurate with its immediate cash needs. This generally means selling stocks and bonds "just in time" to meet cash needs.

New contributions to the Fund should be applied to, and payments by the Fund withdrawn from, asset classes in such a way as to bring the Fund's asset allocation toward its Policy Allocation. If these actions are insufficient to return the portfolio to its Policy Allocation, then the Fund should make additional transactions to rebalance the portfolio at least once a year.

Liquid Assets. The term "liquid assets" includes all investments that the Fund can convert to cash within a year, such as marketable securities, both equity and fixed income.

The Fund should consider investing in all liquid asset classes in which it can gain competency to invest, and it should base its portfolio weight in each class on whatever combination it expects will provide optimal risk/return characteristics for the aggregate portfolio. Where feasible, the Fund should also seek diversification within asset classes. For example, in common stocks, the Fund should normally

TABLE 3.1 Benchmark Portfolio

	Asset Class	Benchmark Index
___%	Large U.S. stocks	Russell 1000 Index
___%	Small U.S. stocks	Russell 2000 Index
___%	Real estate investment trusts	NAREIT Equity Index
___%	Large non-U.S. stocks	MSCI World Index, ex U.S.
___%	Small non-U.S. stock	MSCI EAFE Small Cap Index
___%	Emerging markets stocks	MSCI Emerging Markets Free Index
___%	Investment grade bonds, 10-year duration	Lehman Government Corp. Long-Term Bond Index
___%	Inflation-linked bonds Index	Barclay's U.S. Inflation Linked Bond Index
___%	High-yield bonds	Chase High Yield Developed Market Index
___%	Emerging markets debt	J. P. Morgan Emerging Markets Bond Plus
___%	Market neutral programs	Treasury bills plus 4%
100%		

seek to have *managers* with different styles. The Fund may therefore hire multiple specialist *managers* in a single asset class.

Illiquid Assets.[5] The term "illiquid assets" includes any investment that the Fund cannot readily convert to cash at fair market value within a year, such as partnerships invested in real estate, venture capital, oil & gas, and timberland.

Each new illiquid investment should be selected on an opportunistic basis so as to improve the overall portfolio diversification and to enhance its return. To subscribe to a new illiquid investment, the Fund should have a realistic expectation that it will provide a materially higher net rate of return than a comparable marketable investment in order to compensate for the risk and inconvenience inherent in illiquidity. A still higher expected return should be required of an illiquid investment to the extent that its underlying risk is greater than that of common stocks.

The attractiveness of a prospective illiquid investment will be enhanced by its expected diversification benefit to the Fund's overall portfolio, that is, the extent to which the key factors affecting its investment returns differ from those that affect the Fund's other investments.

No single commitment to an illiquid investment should normally exceed __%[6] of the Fund's total assets. Such commitments are much smaller than commitments the Fund typically makes to *managers* of liquid assets. This is because a great diversity of private asset classes and managers, including time diversification, is desirable due to the illiquid and often specialized nature of private investments.

The success of the Fund's illiquid investments will depend on the extent that, over time, its portfolio of illiquid investments either (a) exceeds the return on the Russell 3000 Index by 3% per year or (b) achieves a net IRR of 15% per year.

Manager Selection and Retention. In every asset class, the Fund's goal is to have its investments managed by the best possible investors that the Fund can access in that asset class. Until such time that the Fund's investment staff can be realistically expected to achieve world-class results in managing any particular asset class (at least equal, net of all costs, to the best the Fund can obtain outside), the day-to-day portfolio management of all Fund investments shall be performed by outside *managers*.

To achieve superior investment returns within the Fund's volatility constraints, the Fund should continuously seek *investment managers* and

---

[5]Small endowment funds probably shouldn't consider illiquid assets.
[6]I'd suggest inserting perhaps 0.5% for a very large fund and 2% for a relatively small fund.

investment opportunities that have expected rates of return higher than those expected from its existing *managers*, especially if this would reduce the Fund's aggregate volatility or improve the manageability of the Fund's overall portfolio.

All *managers*—both prospective and existing—should be evaluated under the following criteria:

- **Character.** Integrity and reliability.
- **Investment approach.** Do the assumptions and principles underlying the *manager's* investment approach make sense to us?
- **Expected return.** The *manager's* historic return, net of fees, overlaid by an evaluation of the predictive value of that historic return, as well as other factors that may seem relevant in that instance and may have predictive value.
- **Expected impact on the Fund's overall volatility.** Two facets:
  a. **Expected volatility**—the historic volatility of the *manager's* investments overlaid by an evaluation of the predictive value of that historic volatility, and recognition of the historic volatility of that *manager's* asset class.
  b. **Expected correlation** of the *manager's* volatility with the rest of the portfolio.
- **Liquidity.** How readily in the future can the account be converted to cash, and how satisfactory is that in relation to the Fund's projected needs for cash?
- **Control.** Can our organization, with the help of its *adviser*, adequately monitor this *investment manager* and its investment program?
- **Legal.** Have all legal concerns been dealt with satisfactorily?

Managers should be selected without regard to the geographic location of their offices and without regard to the nature of their ownership except as those factors may impact the above considerations.

In each asset class, unless it is viable for the Fund to select active *managers* whom it expects, with high confidence, to add meaningful excess long-term value (net of fees and expenses) above their benchmark, then the Fund should invest its assets in an index fund.

Criteria applicable to the selection of an index fund *manager* include that of character and integrity and the *manager's* historic performance (net of fees, taxes, and transaction costs) relative to the respective index.

This sample statement of investment policies contains a number of concepts we may not have discussed adequately. Let's address them now.

The opening statement about "exclusive benefit" and the next—of making all scheduled payments to the fund sponsor without fail—are a bit of motherhood and apple pie, but I think they are so basic that any policy statement should begin with something like them.

Liquidity requirements are necessary to meet the first objective. That statement, however, serves best to remind us that we have great flexibility. The minimum-liquidity requirement allows vastly more illiquid investments than are held by any *investment fund* I am aware of.

The goal of broad diversification is embodied in the range of asset classes that are included in the policy statement. The particular asset classes our plan selects may differ from those in the sample statement, but they should in any case be broadly diversified.

In the calculation of quarterly returns on the Benchmark Portfolio, why would we benchmark illiquid investments against themselves?! Rarely is there a good way to measure quarterly returns on an illiquid asset. The quarterly valuations on these assets often tend to show little movement over time and then incur a sudden change that can obfuscate relative returns on our liquid assets. Returns on illiquid assets certainly need to be benchmarked! But we will profit most by benchmarking their aggregate internal rates of return, over multiyear intervals, against the hurdle rate of return below which, on an expected basis, we wouldn't have chosen to invest in those asset classes.

It is important to establish return and diversification criteria for Illiquid Assets. We should certainly require higher returns from private investments than from liquid assets. And when we find a private opportunity that strikes us as the greatest thing we've ever seen, we need, in order to control our own enthusiasm, a constraint on the maximum percentage of assets we should commit to that opportunity, because we can't change our mind.

If our *investment fund* is small, much less than $100 million, we may want to avoid illiquid investments altogether and omit any reference to them in our policy statement.

In evaluating our returns on Liquid Assets, we should remember we are long-term investors. We must measure quarterly results, but let's not get hung up on them. Our focus should be on results relative to benchmark over the last 5 or 10 years.

The target of minimizing short-term fixed income assets is worth articulating, as most pension and endowment funds tend to retain more cash equivalents than they should.

The paragraph about using contributions and withdrawals to rebalance toward the Policy Asset Allocation codifies our commitment to rebalance our portfolio back to its Policy Allocation as market action drives it away from that allocation. Rebalancing is a critical concept we will cover in detail in Chapter 6.

Our policy statement of using contributions and withdrawals to rebalance implies that this might be done more or less mechanically, without judging what asset classes are attractive or unattractive at the time. That's exactly what I mean to imply! There are few if any mortals who can time asset classes. The sentence takes judgment out of a decision where judgment isn't likely to add value. Also, as mentioned before, it is the lowest-transaction-cost method of rebalancing.

As part of these criteria, we should aim to use the best possible *managers* that we can access in each asset class. That is obviously an unreachable target, but that's the direction in which we should always be striving. I also think we should include a statement about in-house management and its rationale, and also about the role of index funds.

Criteria for *manager* selection and retention are helpful as guideposts against which future *manager* recommendations should be evaluated. We'll discuss more about this in Chapter 5 on selecting *investment managers*.

IN SHORT

- Every *investment fund* should have a written statement of investment objectives. The statement sets directions and criteria that will help to focus everyone who will be involved in subsequent decisions.
- We should first establish the time horizon for our portfolio (usually very long term), then how much risk, or volatility, we can afford. Our target rate of return should then be "the highest we can achieve without exceeding our target level of volatility."
- Our statement of investment objectives should include our Policy Asset Allocation as well as benchmarks against which we can measure the success of our investment program.

CHAPTER 4

Asset Allocation

By far, the most important single investment decision that our *investment fund* makes is not the particular *investment managers* we select, but our asset allocation. That's the proportion of our total assets we put into each asset class, such as large U.S. stocks, long-term bonds, or real estate equity. Asset allocation determines up to 90% of our future investment returns.

If we think first of *manager* selection, we are implicitly making allocations to asset classes. Why? Because investment results within an asset class are so dominated by the wind behind that asset class,[1] any *manager's* results will be highly impacted by that wind. If large U.S. stocks achieve high returns, so will nearly all *managers* of large U.S. stocks; and those *managers* will not be able to escape the slaughter if large U.S. stocks should crash.

Historically, many *endowment funds* have drifted toward an asset allocation something like 60/30/10, that is, 60% in stocks, 30% in bonds, and 10% in cash equivalents, all U.S. based. Is there something inherently ideal in that asset mix? If there is, it isn't apparent in other countries, where typical asset allocation differs greatly from country to country.

Which nation's conventional investment wisdom is best? The overwhelming reason for each fund's asset allocation is . . . that's how it's always done here. Fund sponsors feel safety in numbers, and many are timid about investing their money differently.

Let's obey all laws diligently. But I suggest that an *investment fund* does well to ignore how its peers are investing their money. Instead, let's set our asset allocation on the basis of (1) our objectives, as discussed in Chapter 3,

---

[1]The "wind," as I call it, means the things that tend to affect the returns of all investments in a particular asset class at any given time.

and (2) after careful study of available information about the financial markets, our independent application of logic and common sense.

CHARACTERISTICS OF AN ASSET CLASS

The trouble is, the very names of asset classes—foreign stocks, small stocks, emerging markets, venture capital—evoke varying emotions that get in the way of rational evaluation by investors. A helpful starting point with any asset class is to describe it quantitatively in order to move as far as possible from the emotional to the intellectual.

To develop our Target Asset Allocation we need to quantify three critically important characteristics of every asset class:

1. Its expected return,
2. Its expected risk, and
3. Its expected correlations with every other asset class.

Why are these characteristics so important? Because they enable us through diversification to accomplish our basic investment objective: the highest net investment return our portfolio can achieve within whatever limit of annual volatility we can accept.

The problem is that essentially riskless assets, such as U.S. Treasury bills, provide the lowest long-term returns. And assets with the highest expected returns, such as start-up venture capital, are the most risky. The risk/return chart in Figure 4.1 shows that the higher the expected rate of return from an asset class is, the higher its volatility tends to be.

To some extent, diversification offers us a way to have our cake and eat it too—to hold more higher-risk, higher-return assets without increasing overall portfolio volatility. By assembling a portfolio of asset classes that march to somewhat different drummers (that have a low correlation with one another), we can increase our portfolio's expected return at any given level of expected volatility. What counts is the portfolio's *aggregate* volatility, not the volatility of each asset or each asset class.

To illustrate, let's look at an imaginary portfolio of only two assets, both having a high expected return of X%, both extremely volatile, but with returns that move exactly opposite to one another—that is, with a correlation of –1. This means when asset A goes up by X + Y%, asset B returns X – Y%, and vice versa. Although each asset is extremely volatile, the aggregate volatility of the portfolio (assuming rebalancing

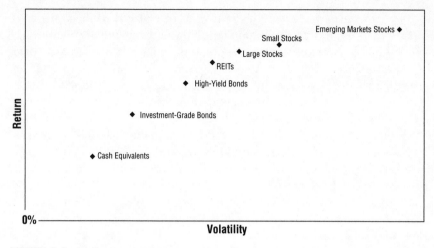

FIGURE 4.1 Risk/Return Chart

each year to 50:50) would be nil—and we would essentially earn X% with no volatility.

Oh, if only two such assets existed! We can't achieve this, but we can get part way by combining asset classes whose annual returns are only partly correlated.

How do we go about quantifying the three key assumptions for each asset class? It's hard. But if we don't do it explicitly, we will end up doing it implicitly and not even recognize what assumptions we are making. Let's discuss these three assumptions—expected return, risk, and correlation.

Wait a minute. As a member of the investment committee, am I expected to come up with these assumptions?

No. For this we must rely on our *adviser*. But the next few paragraphs will enable us to ask questions that will help us understand how our assumptions are being developed.

Expected Investment Return

By return, we mean the compound annual net return we expect over the next 10 to 20 years. Why not the return we expect over the next year or two? Because I don't think anyone can forecast short-term results. Then, how do we forecast long-term returns?

We can start by studying historical returns, placed in the context of valuations now and at the beginning of the interval we are measuring. Large U.S. stocks, for example, have about the most reliable historical data of any asset class. Ibbotson Associates *Yearbook*[2] goes back to 1926 in providing the total investment return (including reinvested dividends) on Standard & Poor's 500 Index—a good index of the performance of large U.S. stocks—and on other U.S. securities.

From 1926 through 2004, the S&P 500 compounded 10.4% per year. That's impressive, as it includes the Depression, World War II, and the terrible investment climate of the 1970s. Does that mean we should expect 10% per year going forward?

Well, let's say we have a 20-year time horizon. What is the range of the S&P's total annual returns over all 20-year intervals? We find it varies from a low of 3% per year for the 1929–1948 interval to a high of 18% per year for the recent interval of 1980–1999. On a real (inflation-adjusted) basis, the range is from a low of 1.6% to a high of 13.6%.

A key question: Should we attribute equal predictive value to all years of available historical data? Or should we say the world has changed materially since 19XX, and we should rely mainly on data since then? Remember, historical data for an asset class (or for a particular *investment manager*) is no more useful than its predictive value, and that's a judgment we must make.

Also, we should consider adjusting our expectations relative to historical returns based on our view of whether stocks are priced dearly or cheaply today. We should recognize, for example, that the phenomenal returns on U.S. stocks for the last 20 years of the twentieth century reflect (1) the fact that corporate earnings grew exceptionally fast over that interval while (2) stock valuations zoomed from a price/earnings ratio of about 8 at year-end 1979 to about 32 by year-end 1999.

As we study history, we might also consider the truism that total return must equal dividend yield plus the rate of earnings-per-share growth, adjusted for change in the price/earnings ratio. Going forward from today, what growth in long-term GDP (Gross Domestic Product) do we expect for the U.S. economy—the combination of real GDP plus inflation? Given that GDP growth, what growth rate do we expect in corporate earnings? In

---

[2]Historical returns on the S&P 500 and certain other U.S. asset classes shown subsequently in this chapter are taken or calculated from Ibbotson Associates' *Stocks, Bonds, Bills and Inflation Yearbook*.

other words, what change do we expect in corporate earnings as a percentage of GDP? Finally, what change, if any, do we expect in the market's price/earnings ratio?

In the final analysis, what should we select as our expected return for large U.S. stocks? No, we can't look to the gurus of Wall Street to tell us, because we will find an impressive guru who will support any expectation we select. Recognize from the start that any return expectation we select will almost surely be wrong! A bull's-eye forecast would be phenomenal luck.

Should we therefore give up? No, because a well-thought-out expectation should get us in the ballpark. This is true of all asset classes, some of which do not have clean historical data going back very far. We should examine whatever data exists and apply our common sense in projecting that data into the future, and then . . . plan on some serious sensitivity tests.

Our purpose in this book is not to provide all the historical data and try to apply it but rather to suggest the kinds of questions we should ask about the relevance of that historical data to our expectations for the future.

Expected Risk

As discussed in Chapter 1, the best measure of risk is the volatility, or standard deviation, of returns. We can measure the volatility of returns of an asset class historically. For example, over the 78 years 1926–2003 the total return on the S&P 500 had a standard deviation of some 20 percentage points. That means that if the average year's return was 13%, and if future returns should be the same, then in roughly two-thirds of the years the S&P 500's return should be about 13% ± 20 percentage points, or between –7% and +33%, and about one-sixth of the years it should be below –7%, and one-sixth of the years above +33%.

This example also suggests that in some 5% of the years, return should be beyond two standard deviations, or 13% ± 40 percentage points. That means below –27% and above +53%.

That's history. But how do we forecast volatility? Do we project historical volatility from the last 78 years (some 20 percentage points), or from the last 20 years (about 17 percentage points), or from some other interval? Again, no one can give us the answer. We must apply our own common sense.

As might be predictable, cash equivalents have very little volatility, investment-grade bonds have relatively low volatility, and stocks are materially more volatile than bonds.

In asset classes where there is little reliable historic information, how do we assess expected volatility? It is not easy. But it is still worth doing.

Expected Correlation

Again, as indicated in Chapter 1, an understanding of correlations can lead to the counterintuitive realization that it is better to make a portfolio less risky by adding a small amount of a risky but uncorrelated security than by adding a conservative but highly correlated security.

As we diversify, each additional asset class does incrementally less to lower our aggregate volatility. Given that fact, then why do I advocate using as many asset classes as possible that have high expected returns? Mainly because I don't believe my own correlation estimates. I suspect that some asset classes we now expect to be highly uncorrelated will become more closely correlated over time, and vice versa. The larger the number of diverse asset classes we invest in, and the less correlated their returns, the more protected we are.

Our task, of course, is to make a reasonable assumption about the correlation for each asset class with every other asset class. For example, if we work with 15 asset classes, we will need a matrix of 105 correlations! Where do we get them?

Historical correlation data is available for some asset classes, mainly through consulting firms at present. For certain asset classes, meaningful correlation data does not exist. We must make a reasoned guess as we relate those asset classes to others for which correlation data is available. Illustrated later in the chapter is a sample table of input assumptions for an Efficient Frontier, including a correlation matrix—but with only illustrative assumptions, not necessarily ones you will want to use.

Do you get the idea we are dealing with some soft projections? You are right. But with proper research and thought, those projections can be good enough to help us develop reasonably optimal asset allocations.

After all our hard work, we must face the fact that our set of assumptions must be wrong. No one has a clear enough crystal ball to get even a single assumption right. Should we therefore forget about these academic prognostications? No! There are important ways to deal with this uncertainty, which we shall address later in this chapter.

ASSET CLASSES

Well, what asset classes should we consider? All of them. Or at least all asset classes that we are competent—or can gain competency—to invest in. Some of the more obvious asset classes include the following.

Cash Equivalents

Cash equivalents (which, for short, we shall call "cash") include Treasury bills, short-term certificates of deposit, money market mutual funds, and short-term investment funds (STIFs)—investments that are usually thought of as riskless, in that their maturity is so short we can hardly lose any of our principal. If we venture outside of U.S. government securities, we may take some credit risk, but for our purposes here let's consider cash as riskless.

If cash is riskless, then we should expect that cash has the lowest expected long-term return—and this has been true through the years. Over the last 79 years, cash has barely returned 1 percentage point more than the inflation rate. For certain intervals of years cash hasn't even returned the inflation rate, but over the 10 years 1995–2004 its return averaged some 1½ percentage points higher than inflation.

We might start our expectations with an estimate of the inflation rate going forward and then decide what increment over that inflation rate cash is likely to return.

And then ask ourselves: If over any long-term interval cash is likely to provide the lowest return, why should we target any portion of our portfolio to cash? Well, cash is a great tool for market timing, but I feel safe in assuming we are not blessed with the gift of prescience.

Many investors keep a portion in cash so that whenever they must withdraw some money from their fund they can do so without having to sell a longer-term security at a possibly inopportune time. Withdrawals, however, occur repeatedly over time. Over the long term, a fund is undoubtedly better off keeping cash to zero and selling other securities whenever a withdrawal is needed—selling "just in time." Sometimes, we'll sell at the bottom of the market and other times at the top. But over the long term, we should be well ahead.

In any case, I favor a target allocation of 0% in cash.[3]

---

[3]No matter how hard we try, it is difficult to keep cash down to zero. Over the long term, any amount of cash is a drag on portfolio return. One way to deal with this, if our fund is large enough and if our cash balances are not too volatile, is to overlay our cash balances with very liquid index futures, such as S&P 500 futures. Such futures "equitize" our cash, effectively converting it into an S&P 500 index fund.

Longer-Term Fixed Income

There are at least six distinct classes of bonds, and we should consider including each:

- Traditional investment-grade bonds
- Long-duration bonds
- Non-U.S. bonds from developed markets
- High-yield bonds
- Emerging markets debt
- Inflation-linked bonds

Traditional Bonds   Traditional investment-grade bonds come in various maturities, typically from one year to 30 years, and various levels of credit risk, each having somewhat different long-term risk and return characteristics. When talking of this asset class, we often talk in terms of the Lehman Aggregate Bond Index, which attempts to include all investment-grade U.S. fixed income securities that are longer in maturity than cash equivalents.

Because the market values of bonds are more volatile than of cash, we would expect a higher return from bonds, long term. In recent years, the yield on U.S. bonds has tended to be a couple of percentage points higher than on cash equivalents. Total returns on bonds during the 79 years through 2004 averaged almost 3% over the inflation rate. Historically, bonds have had a modest annual correlation with stocks.

It is difficult to find an active *manager* of traditional investment-grade U.S. bonds who can add as much as 1 percentage point of excess net return above his benchmark. The other classes of bonds offer active *managers* the opportunity to add a little more excess return above their benchmarks—*if* the *managers* are among the best.

Long-Duration Bonds   Unless we think interest rates are going to decline (usually a gambler's bet), why would we want to consider investing in highly volatile long-duration bonds—much less as a replacement for traditional bonds? One possible reason is that the volatility of a long-duration bond account can give us more protection against declining interest rates than a traditional bond account, especially in a climate such as occurred in the third quarter of 1998, when stock prices collapsed at the same time that interest rates declined.

For this reason, long-duration bonds reduce our need to allocate as large a percentage of our portfolio to fixed income, which historically has provided a lower long-term rate of return than equity investments.

Pension funds have a reason to be especially interested in long-term bonds. We'll discuss this in Chapter 10, "What's Different About Pension Funds."

Non-U.S. Bonds (Developed Countries)   While the U.S. government and U.S. corporations are the world's largest issuers of public debt, government and corporate bonds are sold to the public in all developed countries of the world. That spells additional opportunity.

When fully hedged for foreign exchange risk, foreign bonds tend to have a fairly high correlation with U.S. bonds. Knowledgeable global investors, however, can find ways to add value, because interest rate movements across countries are certainly not in perfect synch.

A global bond portfolio that is not hedged provides more diversification benefit. The difference is volatility in foreign exchange values, which is largely uncorrelated with the volatility in bonds and stocks.

Perhaps, rather than adding non-U.S. bonds from developed markets as a separate asset class, the most practical approach may be to allow our bond *manager* (or *managers*) to invest opportunistically anywhere in the developed world that they believe will strengthen their long-term return.

High-Yield Bonds   During the 1980s, high-yield bonds were introduced to finance less creditworthy companies. Known for some years as junk bonds, they are bonds with a high interest rate, with interest rates 1% to 4% higher than investment-grade bonds, sometimes much higher yet for bonds with the lowest credit rating. The higher interest rates are designed to compensate investors for a small percentage of the issuers who statistically can be predicted to default.

High-yield bonds provided investors with moderately higher long-term returns than investment-grade bonds, and for the seven years 1992–1998 they did it with roughly the same volatility. Those, however, were good economic times. During harder economic times, as in 1990 and 2000–2002, many issuers of high-yield bonds defaulted, and prices of high-yield bonds tumbled.

Until recently, almost all high-yield bonds were issued by U.S. corporations. Now, European companies have begun to issue high-yield bonds also.

Emerging Markets Debt   Some people consider debt issued in the developing countries of the world simply another facet of high-yield bonds. There appears to be only a modest correlation, however, between high-yield bonds and emerging markets debt, because their fundamentals are driven by somewhat different factors. Therefore, I tend to view them separately. Most emerging markets debt consists of bonds of sovereign countries, but increasingly, bonds of certain private corporations are becoming investable.

Notwithstanding a collapse in prices of emerging markets debt after Russia defaulted on its bonds in August 1998, emerging markets debt over the 10 years 1995–2004 delivered double-digit total returns. That's common stock territory. If we can stand the volatility with a small portion of our portfolio, I like emerging markets debt. I think it will provide relatively strong returns long term, and returns that have a low correlation with more traditional assets.

Inflation-Linked Bonds   These are mainly government bonds that promise a real return (above the inflation rate) until maturity. Inflation-linked bonds were first introduced by the United Kingdom in the early 1980s. The United States introduced them in 1997, and they are known here as Treasury Inflation-Protected Securities (TIPS). Other countries that have issued inflation-linked bonds include Sweden, Canada, France, Australia, and New Zealand.

Investors who hold the bonds to maturity have a locked-in real return of typically 1 to 4% or more, depending on their purchase price. Meanwhile the bonds fluctuate in value but not normally as much as traditional bonds. One advantage is that they may be correlated slightly negatively with traditional bonds—that is, when regular bond prices go up, prices of inflation-linked bonds may tend to go down, and vice versa.

Common Stocks

Large U.S. Stocks   Large U.S. stocks have been the least volatile stocks in the world. We've talked a bit about large U.S. stocks earlier in this chapter, but now let's compare their returns with those of bonds.

There hasn't been a 20-year interval in the last 70 years when bonds provided a higher rate of return than stocks. Such historical results also square with good old common sense. After all, unless we had a rational expectation that stocks would give us a materially higher return, why would we buy a stock whose future price could be anything, high or low, when we could buy a bond that we can redeem at par value (usually $1,000) X years from now? For the long term, unless investors en masse are irrational, we have to expect a materially higher return from stocks than from bonds. The key question is—how much higher?

Over the 79 years through 2004, the S&P 500—a measure mainly of the largest stocks—returned $4^1/_2$ percentage points per year more than bonds and over 7 points more than inflation.[4] My guess is that in the years ahead, both the real return on stocks and the return differential between stocks and bonds will be distinctly smaller than they have been heretofore. Even so, the return differential over the long term should still be material.

Stocks of any size are often arbitrarily divided between categories of growth and value stocks. No one quite agrees on the precise quantitative definitions of "growth" and "value," but in general, stocks with higher earnings growth rates are categorized as growth and those with low price-to-book-value ratios are categorized as value.

There are multiple indexes of growth and value stocks, and while each is a little different, all show that growth and value tend to move in somewhat different cycles. Unless we recognize this, we might regard all *managers* of growth stocks as brilliant during some intervals, and as dunces during other intervals (and vice versa for value *managers*). Obviously, we must understand a *manager's* style to evaluate him properly.

For diversification in our asset allocation, we should probably have both growth and value *managers*.

Small U.S. Stocks　　Step one is to define small stocks. The Russell 2000 index defines them by market capitalization, as the 2,000 largest U.S. stocks *after* eliminating the largest 1,000 stocks, rebalanced annually.[5] The largest 1,000 U.S. stocks (measured by the Russell 1000) account for some 90% of the total market capitalization of U.S. stocks; the Russell 2000 for another $8^1/_2$%; and some 8,000 tinier stocks (which we might refer to as microcaps) account for the final $1^1/_2$%.

Small U.S. stocks are often treated as a separate asset class, because over the years they have at times had quite different returns from large

---

[4]These figures overstate the advantage of stocks to some extent. In 1926, at the beginning of the 78-year interval, stocks sold at prices that provided an average dividend yield of more than 5%. Today, prices have risen so high that the average dividend yield is scarcely 2%. That decline couldn't happen again from today's dividend yield. If the market's dividend yield and price/earnings ratio had remained unchanged over the years (and that might be the best we can expect going forward from today), then the 78-year annual return on the S&P 500 would have been well below 10%—barely 3% more than the return on bonds and about $5^1/_2$% above inflation.

[5]As of May, 2004, the Russell organization reconstituted the Russell 2000 index (as it does annually) to include companies with market caps between $176 and $1,600 million. But, of course, by the time the reconstituted index was put in place on June 25, market price changes had materially widened the range of market caps.

stocks. From 1979, when the Russell 2000 index was created, through 2004, its annual rate of return lagged that of the S&P 500 by 0.4%/year. Over the 78 years 1926 through 2003, Ibbotson data shows that small stocks (defined differently from and materially smaller than the Russell 2000) returned more than 2 percentage points per year more than the S&P 500. But much of this excess return was earned in a single 10-year interval, under conditions unlikely to be repeated. Based on the Ibbotson data, witness the cycles shown in Table 4.1.

What expectation is most rational for us to make going forward?

Individual small stocks have been a lot more volatile than large stocks, and even a broad portfolio of small stocks like the Russell 2000 has averaged several percentage points more in annual volatility than large stocks. The correlation has been low enough, however, that a mixture of, say, 20% small stocks with the balance in large stocks would have had a slightly lower volatility than a portfolio of large stocks alone.

Because investment analysts don't follow small stocks as widely as larger stocks, a good *manager* of small stocks should be able to add more value to an index of small stocks than a good *manager* of large stocks can add to an index of large stocks. The flip side, of course, is that a below-average *manager* of small stocks is more likely to get bagged!

As with large stocks, the use of both growth and value small-stock *managers* can add useful diversification.

Possibly a separate category is microcap stocks—stocks smaller than those in the Russell 2000 index. It is hard to get much money into microcap stocks because they are simply too small. To the extent it is possible, however, microcap stocks act as a further diversifying element, since they behave somewhat differently from Russell 2000 stocks. They have much higher volatility and transaction costs, but if we can stand the volatility, a strong manager can earn good returns from them.

TABLE 4.1   Annual Rates of Return for Stocks over Different Time Periods

No. of Years	Interval	S&P 500	Small Stocks	Advantage of Small Stocks
34	1926–59	10.3%	10.5%	+ 0.2 points
8	1960–67	9.6	19.5	+ 9.9
6	1968–73	3.5	−5.6	− 9.1
10	1974–83	10.6	28.4	+17.8
15	1984–98	17.9	11.0	− 6.9
5	1999–2003	−0.6	16.3	+16.9

Mid-Cap U.S. Stocks   Some *investment funds* include midcap stocks as an additional asset category. There are multiple definitions of mid-cap stocks, but basically they are ones larger than those in the Russell 2000 index, perhaps as large as $10 to $15 billion in market cap. They do have somewhat different characteristics from large or small stocks, and they're not quite as volatile as small stocks. But, relative to large stocks, they don't provide as much diversification benefit as small stocks.

Real Estate Investment Trusts (REITs)   REITs are a form of common stock. They trade on stock exchanges but, unlike regular corporations, they pay no income tax. They pass their income tax liability on to their shareholders, which is just fine for a taxfree *investment fund*. To qualify for such tax treatment, an REIT must meet specific legal criteria, such as earning 75% of its gross income from rents or mortgage interest, and distributing 90% of each year's taxable income to shareholders.

REITs have been around for more than 30 years, but for a long time they were small in number, with a sizable proportion devoted to investing in high-risk construction lending. The number of REITs devoted to owning properties has mushroomed since the early 1990s, and their aggregate value has gone up more than 20 times. Yet today, they may own little more than 5% of total commercial real estate in the United States. Some industry observers expect that eventually REITs will own the majority of commercial properties in the country. Some REITs are private, but most are publicly traded.

Why distinguish REITs from any other U.S. common stock? Although to some extent they share in stock market cycles, their returns are driven by commercial real estate values, whose cycles have a low correlation with those of the stock market.

Should we rely on our regular common stock *managers* to invest in REITs, or should we hire a specialist in REITs? Because investing in marketable REITs requires a lot more real estate savvy than most *investment managers* have, and requires lots more research about the particular properties owned by each individual REIT, I favor an REIT specialist *manager*. And because REITs may have only a .4 correlation with the S&P 500, I favor treatment of REITs as a separate asset class in our Policy Asset Allocation.

Non–U.S. Stocks   Unlike Scottish investors, who have been global investors for nearly 200 years, U.S. investors have until relatively recent years been among the more provincial. They implicitly assumed that appropriate investment opportunities began and ended in the United States even though the total value of U.S. stocks has for much of the last 20 years been below half of the total value of all stocks in the world (although by year-end 2003 U.S. stocks again comprised about half of the world's market cap).

Some U.S. investors have now moved 20% or more of their equity portfolios outside the United States—and for good long-term reasons. It is hard to argue that expected returns from stocks in the developed countries of the world should be materially different from those in the United States. For the full 34-year interval 1971–2004 since the MSCI EAFE index was started, their returns were about the same. But differences over shorter intervals have been dramatic!

For example, during the four years from 1985 to 1988 stocks of the developed countries outside the U.S. outperformed U.S. stocks by 26 percentage points per year. Then for the next 13 years (1989–2001) U.S. stocks outperformed by 11 points per year. We don't need to calculate a correlation coefficient to see that U.S. and non–U.S. stocks have provided real diversification for one another.

U.S. investors often worry that foreign currencies will lose value relative to the dollar. On the other hand, foreign currencies can be an opportunity as well as a risk. Overall, from the beginning to the end of the 33 years from 1970 to 2003, changes in foreign exchange values had very little impact on investment returns—despite substantial impact during shorter intervening intervals.

If investors are unduly worried about foreign exchange risk, they can always hedge that risk through the purchase of foreign exchange futures. I am not much inclined, however, to spend my money on such an "insurance policy" unless a very large percentage of our portfolio is at foreign-exchange risk. In any case, foreign exchange risk is not a reason to avoid considering non–U.S. investments.

David Swensen of Yale refers to diversification as a "free lunch."[6] In a simplistic way, non–U.S. stocks can be used to illustrate the point. Even though the non–U.S. EAFE stock index had a slightly lower return and was more volatile than the S&P 500 during the 30-year interval from 1970 to 1999, a portfolio consisting of 40% EAFE and 60% S&P would have provided a slightly higher return than the S&P 500 alone, and at a volatility nearly 2 percentage points per year lower.[7] A modest allocation to highly volatile emerging markets stocks would have made this simple portfolio more efficient yet.

---

[6]Swensen, *Pioneering Portfolio Management* (The Free Press, 2000), p. 67.
[7]Source: Ibbotson Associates.

Small Non–U.S. Stocks   Small stocks outside the U.S. offer further diversification value. Just as in the United States, their returns have had materially different patterns from large stocks. Likewise, small stocks outside the U.S. have had lengthy intervals of materially outperforming and underperforming large stocks.

From country to country, the correlations among small-stock returns are substantially lower than the correlations among large-stock returns. Within each country, of course, small stocks are considerably more volatile than large stocks. But because of the low country correlations, the MSCI EAFE Small Stock index is only marginally more volatile than the large stock MSCI EAFE index.

The comments earlier in this chapter about growth and value relative to U.S. stocks apply equally to non–U.S. stocks, both large and small.

Emerging Markets Stocks   With the rapid spread of private enterprise among the less-developed countries of the world, especially since the end of the Cold War, a new asset class has come about. Stocks of Singapore, Hong Kong, and the less-developed countries now account for some 10% of the value of the world's common stocks.

Over the last dozen years or more, the GNP of a number of those countries has been growing at a rate of 5% to 10% per year, compared with 2% to 4% for the developed economies. Hence, there is reason to expect companies in the emerging markets to grow faster and their stocks to provide a greater return than in the developed world—especially if the accounting and shareholder orientation of those companies continue to improve.

But what about their volatility? It is not at all unusual to see the aggregate return on stocks in a particular developing country go up by 100% in a year or down by 50%—or more. If we could invest only in a single developing country, the risk would be tremendous. But today we can invest in some 60 developing countries, and over time their returns have had a relatively low correlation with one another. Stocks in one country may be way up when those in another country go into a tailspin. Indexes of emerging markets stocks are composed of 25 to 30 different countries, and these diversified indexes—while still a lot more volatile than those of the developed world—still have low enough volatility to be fruitfully considered by institutional investors.

Emerging markets stock indexes provide a good example of the advantage of low correlations. On average, the volatility of the stock market of individual developing countries may be well over 40 percentage points per year, but taking all countries together, the volatility of the emerging markets has been in the range of 25 to 30 percentage points.

Tactical Asset Allocation (TAA)

In the mid-1980s, a number of managers developed complex computer programs that moved assets unemotionally back and forth between stock and bond index funds, depending on which seemed to their quantitative models the most attractively valued at the time. These Tactical Asset Allocation programs are now sometimes invested entirely through index futures, because futures are most cost-efficient. And the models have now become increasingly sophisticated, using futures for different sizes of U.S. stocks, and futures for stock and bond markets of more than 15 countries outside the United States.

Because of their quantitative models, TAA managers can readily tailor their products to whatever mandate—or benchmark—a client might prefer, such as the MSCI World stock index, or 50% S&P 500/50% Lehman Aggregate, or any other index or combination of indexes. What counts, of course, is their risk-adjusted returns relative to their benchmarks.

So how have they done? Well, there are differences among TAA managers, of course, but on average they have not tended to outperform their benchmarks nor to keep their volatility measurably below their benchmarks.

If we want at least one of our accounts to vary its asset allocation tactically, a TAA account may be our best choice, if we are able to select a TAA manager who in the future can achieve above-average returns. Use of an experienced TAA manager may at least be a better way to vary our asset allocation tactically than doing it intuitively based on our own predilections or those of our *adviser*.

Alternative Asset Classes

In the minds of many investors, the concept of asset allocation ends with traditional marketable securities. Perhaps they might identify real estate as another viable asset class. But we can strengthen our portfolio materially with additional asset classes, such as:

Start-up venture capital funds

Leveraged buyout funds

Corporate buy-in funds

Distressed securities

Oil and gas properties

Timberland

Market neutral funds, such merger and acquisition arbitrage and convertible arbitrage

Hedge funds (funds that may be short some common stocks while also holding a long equity portfolio)

Commodity Futures (Including Foreign Exchange)

We shall discuss these asset classes in some detail in Chapter 5. But for now, let's just consider how we go about estimating future returns, volatility, and correlations.

With arbitrage programs or hedge funds, where the skill of the manager is more important than the asset class itself, the particular manager's historic returns may be useful indicators. Asset classes that add great diversification benefit to a portfolio are those that are market neutral—whose correlation with the stock market is close to zero. Many arbitrage strategies get down to correlations of 0.3 or less. Also close to zero correlation are many long/short common stock funds whose short positions are equal in value to their long positions.

When it comes to illiquid investments, such as real estate or venture capital, estimating their volatility and correlation with other asset classes is harder yet. The "market" values at which we carry these assets on our books are much less meaningful because each asset is unique. No identical asset is being bought and sold every day in the marketplace. Valuations are established by (1) judgmental appraisals, as with real estate, or (2) the price at which the last shares of a stock were sold, even if that was two years ago, or (3) the book value of the investment, which is the usual valuation of a private investment in which there have been no transactions, perhaps for years, or (4) a written-down value if the manager has strong evidence that an investment's value has been impaired.

Given these approaches to valuation, illiquid investments often appear to have materially less volatility than common stocks. But note the emphasis on the word "appear." The price at which a particular investment could be sold certainly goes up and down each quarter—undoubtedly with great volatility for a start-up venture, for example—even though its reported value is kept unchanged quarter after quarter.

Which volatility of an illiquid investment should we assess—the volatility of its reported returns or the estimated volatility of its underlying returns?

In the reports we make on our investment fund, we have to base our returns on reported valuations. But let's stop and consider two investments: a marketable stock and a start-up venture capital stock. Let's say each is sold after seven years and each returned 16% per year over that interval. Which was the more volatile?

The marketable stock had lots of ups and downs, whereas the venture capital stock was kept at book value much of the time. Was the marketable stock more volatile? If our time horizon for measuring volatility is seven years, we could say they had the same volatility. But there was obviously a lot greater uncertainty as to the seven-year return on the venture capital stock than on the marketable stock. The underlying annual volatility of the venture capital stock had to have been a lot higher.

We could make a good case that our expected volatility of an illiquid investment should reflect the innate uncertainty in its return—that is, its underlying volatility.

Next, how does one assess correlations between liquid and illiquid investments? We should study whatever data we have, but ultimately we'll have to go with an educated guess.

PUTTING IT ALL TOGETHER

Perhaps with the help of our *adviser*, we have developed a diverse range of assumptions for the return, volatility, and correlation for each of the asset classes we are going to consider. What do we do now?

Why Not 100 Percent Equities

A question that has long bugged me is: Why not 100% equities? If we agree that we should be very long-term oriented, and if we are convinced that over any 20-year interval stocks should outperform bonds, then why not target 100% stocks?

Well, the roller coaster ride of the stock market could be very upsetting. The worst eventuality would be if, at the bottom of a bear market, the stomach of some future investment committee weakened and the committee reduced the allocation to common stocks at that time. So how can we ease the roller coaster ride a little but not impair expected returns unduly?

At this point, I would like to introduce my personal definition of the term "equities." By equities I mean all investments whose expected returns are generally as high as, or higher than, common stocks. I am big on diversification and believe in reducing the volatility of our aggregate portfolio through diversification. But I am convinced that strong diversification can be achieved without resorting to large allocations to assets whose expected returns we believe are materially below that of equities—such as traditional fixed income.

Judicious use of fixed income might let us boost our aggregate return per unit of risk, but unless we can leverage our overall portfolio (and that's tough to do), we can't spend risk-adjusted returns. If we are truly long-term oriented, why not accept a little higher volatility in exchange for higher returns?

Before relegating fixed income to oblivion, let's ask what purpose fixed income should serve in a portfolio, and how best we can fulfill that purpose. For an endowment fund or foundation, traditional investment-grade fixed income serves two key purposes:

1. Traditional fixed income lowers the expected volatility of the portfolio. This is the most common purpose of fixed income, and the purpose I would hope to achieve instead through the use of diverse asset classes that have materially higher expected returns than fixed income.

2. Fixed income gives the portfolio needed strength whenever interest rates decline and stock prices decline at the same time, as in a recession—or heaven forbid, in a depression. No asset class serves this function as well as fixed income.

So maybe there is a bona fide rationale for fixed income, after all. If we must use fixed income with a lower expected return to fulfill purpose 2 above, how can we do it most efficiently? The answer, it seems to me, is in long-duration high-quality bonds. This approach will (1) give us the maximum protection for the economic scenarios where we need protection most and (2) enable us to reduce materially the size of our allocation to lower-expected-return assets.[8]

For pension funds, bonds serve a further crucial purpose, which we shall cover in our final chapter, "What's Different About Pension Funds?"

---

[8]Another approach is to use interest-rate futures combined with market-neutral programs—programs that have little or no correlation with other investments in our portfolio. This approach is called Portable Alpha and will be covered in Chapter 5.

This discussion, however, focuses only on one aspect of asset allocation. Let's now describe a tool that can be immensely helpful as we approach that all-important decision about our fund's Policy Asset Allocation—a tool known as the "Efficient Frontier."

The Efficient Frontier

The Efficient Frontier is a computer-generated single portfolio that will give us the highest expected return for any given level of expected volatility (the expected standard deviation of annual returns from the portfolio's average return). An Efficient Frontier looks like Figure 4.2.

Point A represents a particular portfolio of asset classes that has an expected volatility of 10% per year. No portfolio of asset classes with the same expected volatility will give an expected return higher than point A. Every point on the curve—the "Efficient Frontier"—represents a different portfolio of asset classes that provides the highest expected return at that level of volatility.

You can see from this graph that at the lowest level of volatility we can increase the expected rate of return rapidly with little increase in the expected portfolio volatility. But the higher the expected rate of return, the more portfolio volatility we must take on to increase still further our ex-

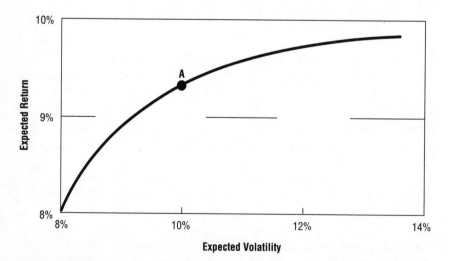

FIGURE 4.2   An Efficient Frontier

pected rate of return. At some point, we can increase portfolio volatility almost without gaining any incremental expected return.

As we consider alternative asset allocations, we should have two objectives:

1. We want to move the Efficient Frontier line as high as possible. As shown by Figure 4.3, the larger the number of diverse asset classes we include in the optimizer the higher the Efficient Frontier line is likely to be—and the higher the expected return we can get at any given volatility level. Note how limited is a portfolio based only on U.S. stocks, high-grade bonds, and cash equivalents. Note also that all 10 asset classes in Figure 4.3 are liquid asset classes. The Efficient Frontier would be higher yet if illiquid asset classes were added.

   The Efficient Frontiers in Figure 4.3 would be different, of course, under different assumptions. But under virtually all reasonable assumptions, the Efficient Frontier based on a larger number of diverse asset classes would be materially higher than an Efficient Frontier based on fewer asset classes. Figure 4.4 compares a well-diversified portfolio with that of an actual endowment fund. It illustrates the advantage of diversification under a range of different assumptions.

2. After moving the Efficient Frontier as high as we can, we then want to develop a Policy Asset Allocation that will get us as close as possible to the Efficient Frontier line at our chosen volatility constraint.

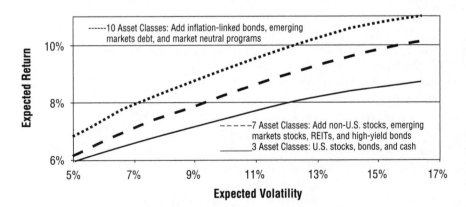

FIGURE 4.3 Alternative Portfolios
The more diverse asset classes we use in our model, the higher the Efficient Frontier.

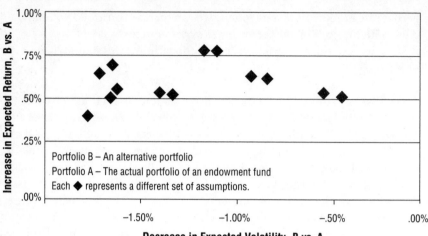

FIGURE 4.4 Sensitivity Tests
Under 13 sets of assumptions, Portfolio B (a more diversified portfolio) provides materially higher expected return and lower volatility than Portfolio A (the current portfolio of an actual endowment fund). The assumptions are combinations of those used by five different consultants.

As our *adviser* inputs his assumptions for the return, volatility, and correlations of each asset class (see the illustration of input assumptions in Table 4.2), he should also enter certain constraints. With no constraints, the optimizer might hypothetically tell us the most efficient portfolio consists of only emerging markets stocks, emerging markets debt, and arbitrage programs!

We wouldn't want more than X% of our portfolio subject to the common factors that periodically infect prices in the emerging markets. And we doubt that we could get more than Y% of our portfolio into quality arbitrage programs. We should go through each of our asset classes and ask ourselves if we need a constraint for that asset class or for any combination of asset classes. We also might consider a requirement to have at least Z% of the portfolio in a particular asset class, such as U.S. stocks. We should limit such constraints and requirements, however, to only those cases where we have a compelling reason. Each such constraint will lower the Efficient Frontier line.

Because any set of assumptions must be wrong, we want our *adviser* to run extensive sensitivity tests by calculating Efficient Frontiers based on a range of assumptions. That way we will eventually home in on asset allocations that are robust—that are least sensitive to a range of reasonable assumptions. If there is one set of asset allocations that seems optimal, what changes in assumptions will make the portfolio suboptimal? What other asset allocations are just about as good but not as sensitive to changes in assumptions?

This is all very technical. As a committee member, what is my role in this Efficient Frontier process?

As committee members, we want to be sure our *adviser* is using an Efficient Frontier model. We can ask questions about how he arrived at his assumptions and why he set constraint levels where he did. We can ask what alternative sets of assumptions he used and what alternative asset allocations seemed about as good as others under his different assumptions.

Use of Efficient Frontier models entails a lot of effort. Many *investment funds* decide their Policy Asset Allocations without going through the Efficient Frontier exercise. But their asset allocations imply certain assumptions for the return, volatility, and correlation of each asset class, and the committee hasn't identified what those assumptions are.

An Even Better Approach to Efficient Frontier

Standard Efficient Frontier computer models give us the most probable result of any particular asset allocation. A more sophisticated Efficient Frontier model, called an Asset/Liability study, uses a Monte Carlo system of 500 or more simulations to give us the range of expected results from each asset allocation—the probability, for example, that in X years time, asset allocation would provide a return higher than Y% (our minimum threshold of pain).

Asset/Liability studies are particularly important for pension funds, as the present value of pension liabilities fluctuates each year as interest rates fluctuate. We will discuss this in more detail in Chapter 10.

But a Monte Carlo simulation can also be useful to endowment funds and foundations. Such simulations can analyze the trade-offs among (a) the highest expected rate of return, (b) the probability of the sponsor suffering reduced income from the endowment fund, and (c) the probability of the endowment fund not maintaining its purchasing power (not keeping up with inflation) through the years.

A Monte Carlo approach, of course, is more expensive and more complex than the standard Efficient Frontier model. For many endowment funds and foundations, the standard Efficient Frontier model may be adequate.

TABLE 4.2 Sample Input: Long-Term Assumptions for Efficient Frontier

	Expected Compound Annual Return	Expected Annual Standard Deviation	Correlations																
			Common Stocks				Fixed Income						Other Assets						
			Large U.S.	Small U.S.	Non-U.S.	Emerging Markets	U.S. Cash Equiv.	U.S. Bonds	Non-U.S. Bonds	25-Year Zeros	High-Yield Bonds	Emerging Mkt. Debt	Core Real Estate	Aggressive RE	Timberland Funds	Private Energy	Private Energy Funds	Distressed Securities	Arbitrage Programs
Common Stocks																			
Large U.S. stocks	7.5%	16%	1.00	.70	.60	.40	-.10	.20	.10	.20	.50	.40	.30	.20	.00	.00	.50	.50	.25
Small U.S. stocks	8.5	19	.70	1.00	.50	.40	-.10	.10	.10	.10	.60	.50	.30	.20	.00	.00	.70	.70	.10
Non-U.S. stocks, developed markets	7.5	19	.60	.50	1.00	.40	.00	.10	.10	.10	.30	.20	.20	.10	.00	.00	.50	.50	.10
Emerging markets stocks	9.5	30	.40	.40	.40	1.00	.00	.10	.10	.10	.20	.50	.20	.00	.20	.20	.10	.10	.00
Fixed Income																			
U.S. cash equivalents	5.0	3	-.10	-.10	.00	.00	1.00	.20	.10	.20	.00	.00	.00	.20	.00	.00	.00	.00	.10
U.S. high-grade bonds	6.0	8	.20	.10	.10	.10	.20	1.00	.80	.80	.40	.40	.00	.10	.10	.00	.20	.10	.10
Non-U.S. bonds, developed markets	6.0	10	.10	.10	.10	.10	.10	.80	1.00	.80	.40	.40	.00	.00	.10	.00	.10	.00	.10

25-year zero-coupon bonds	6.0	32	.20	.10	.10	.10	.20	.80	.80	.40	1.00	.40	.40	.00	.10	.10	.00	.20	.10	.10
High-yield bonds	7.5	12	.50	.60	.30	.20	.50	.40	.40	.40	.40	1.00	.40	.10	.00	.10	.10	.10	.30	.00
Emerging markets debt	8.0	20	.40	.50	.20	.50	.00	.40	.40	.40	.40	.40	1.00	.00	.00	.10	.10	.10	.10	.00
Other Assets																				
Core real estate	7.5	10	.30	.30	.20	.20	.20	.00	.00	.00	.00	.10	.00	1.00	.80	.00	.00	.20	.20	.00
Value-added real estate	9.0	15	.20	.20	.10	.00	.20	.10	.00	.10	.10	.00	.00	.80	1.00	.00	.00	.20	.20	.00
Timberland funds	9.0	15	.00	.00	.00	.20	.00	.10	.10	.10	.10	.10	.10	.00	.00	1.00	.30	-.10	-.10	.00
Private energy properties	9.0	20	.00	.00	.00	.20	.00	.00	.00	.00	.00	.10	.10	.00	.00	.30	1.00	-.10	-.10	.30
Private equity funds*	10.0	25	.50	.70	.50	.10	.00	.20	.10	.20	.20	.10	.10	.20	.20	-.10	-.10	1.00	.30	.00
Distressed securities	9.0	20	.50	.70	.50	.10	.00	.10	.00	.10	.10	.30	.10	.20	.20	-.10	-.10	.30	1.00	.00
Arbitrage programs	9.2	11	.25	.10	.10	.00	.10	.10	.10	.10	.10	.00	.00	.00	.00	.00	.30	.00	.00	1.00

*Includes venture capital, LBO funds, and buy-in funds, both U.S. and non-U.S. Some of these subclasses may not be highly correlated with one another, so it might be advantageous to treat them separately.

A Secondary Benefit of Diversification

Gaining the benefits of diversification is what this chapter is all about. Everyone understands that diversification reduces the aggregate volatility of our portfolio. Fewer people recognize that, in addition, diversification can actually add a little to our expected return! How?

The Efficient Frontier model lets us use our expected returns, standard deviations, and correlations for each asset class to project our portfolio's expected return and standard deviation over the next 10 years. We shall see that the expected volatility of the portfolio can be materially lower than the weighted average volatilities of each of the asset classes, and the expected return of the portfolio can be slightly higher.

Table 4.3 shows a portfolio with an extremely volatile allocation to very long duration bonds. Don't get hung up on the particular assumptions of expected return and expected standard deviation for each asset class. Note instead, at the bottom of the table, the weighted average expected standard deviation is 21.0% whereas the expected standard deviation for the overall portfolio, thanks to diversification, is only 12.5%.

Note also that the weighted average expected return from our 13 asset classes is 8.3%, whereas the expected return on the overall portfolio is 9.6%.[9] That's real diversification benefit!

Of course, our assumptions are wrong. No such assumptions can be right. But change them as we will, the expected volatility and return for the overall portfolio will still be dramatically better than the weighted average volatility and return of our 13 individual asset classes.

A Drawback of Diversification

The kind of broadly diversified portfolio this chapter is leading us to should provide strong long-term returns. But over shorter intervals it may be greatly out of step with results of our peer *investment funds*, which typically invest predominantly in large U.S. stocks. In 1997–1998, for example, the only strong asset class was large U.S. stocks, which returned over 30%, while returns on a broadly diversified portfolio would have been in the lower teens. If we are to invest confidently in a broadly diversified portfolio, we must avoid undue concern about returns achieved by our peers.

---

[9]The calculation assumes that the portfolio will be annually rebalanced to this Policy Asset Allocation. Rebalancing can add a little to the expected return of the overall portfolio.

TABLE 4.3 Illustration of Diversification Benefit

Percent Allocation	Asset Class	Expected Compound Return	Expected Standard Deviation
15%	Large U.S. stocks	8.0%	17%
11%	Small U.S. stocks	8.5	19
12%	Non-U.S. stocks, developed markets	8.0	19
8%	Emerging markets stocks	9.5	30
15%	25-year zero-coupon bonds	6.6	32
2.5%	High-yield bonds	8.0	12
3.5%	Emerging markets debt	8.2	20
7.5%	Value-added real estate	9.0	15
2.5%	Timberland funds	9.0	15
2%	Private energy properties	9.0	20
9%	Private equity funds	9.3	25
4%	Distressed securities	9.0	11
8%	Arbitrage programs	9.2	11
100%			
	Weighted average	*8.3%*	*21.0%*
	Overall portfolio	9.6	12.5

Returns on a broadly diversified portfolio in the first few years of the twenty-first century could have enabled a broadly diversified portfolio to materially outperform typical peer portfolios over longer intervals including 1997–1998.

IN SHORT

■ We should familiarize ourselves with the full range of asset classes in which our portfolio might invest. This range far exceeds traditional ones of domestic stocks, bonds, and cash.

■ To the extent we make use of all the attractive asset classes we can, such diversification can meaningfully reduce our portfolio's volatility and can even ratchet up our expected return.

■ Use of an Efficient Frontier model can help us develop an asset allocation that is likely to give us the best return at any given level of risk.

CHAPTER **5**

Alternative Asset Classes

When we talk about investing, we all too quickly think of stocks and bonds. We fail to think about many other kinds of viable—and valuable—alternative asset classes.

An alternative asset class might be considered any asset class that our decision makers have not considered before. For some, any stocks but the largest, most prestigious U.S. stocks might be an alternative asset class. For purposes of this chapter, however, we shall define alternative asset classes as anything other than marketable stocks, bonds, and cash equivalents.

Under that definition, the Commonfund Benchmark Study found in a survey of 563 U.S. educational endowment funds that 23% of their aggregate assets in fiscal 2000 was allocated to alternative investments.

We shall divide this chapter between two kinds of alternative assets— (a) liquid investments, ones that are often lumped together under the catch-all term "hedge funds," and (b) illiquid investments.

> *As an investment committee member, do I have to know all about these arcane alternative investments?*

No, but I should at least be familiar with what they are so that I can recognize them if our *adviser* recommends an investment in one of them. We have included discussion about each of these kinds of investments in this chapter also as a reference whenever one of these investments comes up for discussion at an investment committee meeting.

LIQUID ALTERNATIVE ASSETS

A valuable addition to most portfolios can be market neutral asset classes—ones that have little or no correlation with stocks and bonds. They are focused on absolute returns, or on returns relative to short-term interest rates.

Arbitrage programs are about the closest to being market neutral. They are especially dependent on the skills of their investor. Arbitrage managers typically buy a portfolio of securities (they go long) and borrow a similar portfolio of securities that they sell (sell short).

As a simplistic example, we might invest $100,000 in General Motors stock and simultaneously borrow $100,000 worth of Ford stock and sell it (sell it short). We would be as long as we are short, and we wouldn't care if the market went up or down, or whether automobile stocks performed well or poorly relative to the market. We would care only about the performance of GM stock relative to the performance of Ford.

Mechanically, such accounts use a sophisticated broker through whom our *manager* buys our long portfolio and then borrows and sells our short portfolio. The lender retains, as collateral, cash slightly exceeding proceeds from the sale of our shorts and invests it in T-bills.[1] Our arbitrage account receives a portion of the interest on the T-bills—as much as 80%, depending on interest rates—and the lender retains the balance as his lending fee and to pay brokerage costs.

Arbitrage accounts take many forms, and we will comment here only on some of the more common ones.

Long/Short Stock Accounts

Nobel laureate Bill Sharpe, a leading proponent of index funds, has said that a long/short strategy is his favorite active strategy.[2]

Conceptually, a long/short stock account is about the simplest arbitrage program—a long stock portfolio, and a short one. Most investors cannot, net of fees, do as well as an index fund, which only buys stocks. A long/short manager has the challenge of adding value both ways—long and short, and he gets no benefit (or harm) from a move in the stock market. Moreover, the fees for a long/short manager, as with all arbitrage managers, are very high—a fixed fee of up to 1% of assets plus, typically, 15% to 20% of net profits above T-bill rates! Obviously, one wants to consider only an exceptional manager for such a task.

---

[1]Short-term U.S. Treasury bills.
[2]Peter J. Tanous, *Investment Gurus*, New York Institute of Finance, 1997, p. 104.

Caveat re short selling: Investors should be aware that short selling incurs risks beyond those of normal long purchases.

- When we buy a stock, we can lose no more than the price of the stock. When we sell a stock short, our losses are unlimited. If the stock doubles in price, we would lose 100%. If it triples in price, we would lose 200%!
- The lender of the shares that we sell short can recall those shares at any time. If we don't return those shares promptly, he can purchase them from the market at our expense. Shrewd traders may see an opportunity to buy shares of a thinly traded stock and drive up the price, and then recall the loaned shares. This is known as a "short squeeze."

Do these risks mean we shouldn't get involved with short selling? No, there can be too much value in short selling. But we do need to be extra confident in the competence of our managers who engage in short selling.

We might think of market-neutral long/short stock managers (ones who are as long as they are short) as being generally one of three kinds:

1. The most conservative kind will take no risk in industries nor perhaps in other common factors. If the investor buys a large pharmaceutical company, he will sell another large pharmaceutical company—betting on the spread between the two pharmaceutical stocks.
2. A second kind won't pair stocks quite so explicitly but will ensure that the aggregate characteristics of his long portfolio (such as price/earnings ratio and earnings growth rates) are the same as those of his short portfolio.
3. The third and most volatile kind tracks how large stocks are priced relative to small stocks, or how "growth stocks" are priced relative to "value stocks," or how one industry is priced relative to another. This manager will buy a basketful of large growth stocks, for example, and sell short a similar-size basketful of small value stocks.

Why is the return of such funds measured against T-bill rates? The long/short fund earns much but not all of the T-bill return through, in effect, the investment of the proceeds from the short sales. Hence, any long/short investor worth his salt should earn more than the T-bill rate.

What should we expect from a long/short stock account? With extremely good long/short stock funds we can earn 4 to 6 percentage points more than T-bill rates. Volatility, while dramatically lower than for a regular common stock account, is still materially higher than for a money-market fund. Correlation with the overall stock market is near zero.

A good long/short stock account should provide better returns than a bond account, with possibly lower volatility and an even lower correlation with the stock market than bonds have with the stock market. A long/short account, like other arbitrage funds, can be used as a Portable Alpha. We'll discuss Portable Alphas after we finish talking about arbitrage programs.

Merger and Acquisition (M&A) Arbitrage

An M&A arbitrage opportunity occurs when Company A bids to buy Company B for $60 a share, compared with Company B's current price of $40. The price of Company B rapidly zooms closely to $60, but not all the way. After all, it is not known whether Company B shareholders will accept that price, or whether the Federal Trade Commission will allow the acquisition. Nor is it known how long it will take for the acquisition to be consummated, if indeed it succeeds in going through. And if the stock market should fall off a cliff, as it did in October 1987, the offer might be withdrawn.

This is where the M&A arbitrageur comes in. He assesses the probabilities that the acquisition will take place and how long it will take, and he offers to buy the stock of Company B for, say, $56 a share. Investors in Company B are pleased with the run-up in price and may sell at that price.[3]

What's in it for the arbitrageur? He buys at $56. If and when the acquisition ultimately takes place he receives $60—a profit of 4/56, or 7%. If the acquisition takes place four months from now, his annualized rate of return is 23% ($1.07^{12/4} - 1$). Sounds easy. But if litigation should drag out the acquisition for a full year, his annualized return is an unsatisfying 7%. And if the deal breaks, and Company A does not acquire Company B after all, then the price of Company B will probably plummet close to its original $40 per share, and our arbitrageur will have lost 16/56, or 29%.

A good arbitrageur does a sophisticated job of assessing the risks of an

---

[3]If the purchase won't be for cash but will instead be for a certain number of Company A shares, then the arbitrageur sells short Company A. That way, the arbitrageur is insulated from market volatility. He is investing only in the spread between the prices of Companies A and B. In such cases, do M&A arbitrageurs need to sell short? They do unless they're willing to take the risks of the stock market.

announced merger plan and thereby performs a useful function that the average common stock manager is not equipped to perform well.

Over the long term, good M&A arbitrageurs may earn net unleveraged returns of 4 to 5% in excess of T-bill rates for their investors. Returns are influenced by the level of T-bill rates, because investment bankers sometimes use the less risky M&A arbitrages as an alternative investment for their money-market accounts. Some arbitrageurs have had negative returns in years when an unusually large number of deals broke (fell apart). A reasonable expectation for the annual volatility of a good unlevered M&A arbitrage program might be roughly 6%—about one-third that of a typical common stock account. The correlation of most M&A arbitrage programs with the stock market may be as high as 0.3.

Convertible Arbitrage

Good money can also be made by buying a convertible bond or convertible preferred stock, whose interest coupon gives it a high yield, and simultaneously selling short the common stock into which the security can be converted. The dividend rate on the common stock would normally provide a much lower yield.

The arbitrageur thus invests in the spread between the interest rate on the convertible and the dividend yield on the stock. But it is more complicated than that. The arbitrageur may earn additional money if the price on the stock declines, because the price of the convertible security is often underpinned by its bond value. Conversely, if a convertible security is priced at a premium above its conversion value (the value of the stock into which it is convertible), and if the issuer of the convertible security should call that security—that is, force its conversion into common stock—the arbitrageur would lose money.

Unfortunately, rates of return on convertible arbitrage are low, perhaps only a few % higher than T-bill rates, unless the program is leveraged, in which case it may provide low double digit returns.

For tax-exempt funds, however, leverage generally results in unrelated business taxable income, which is taxable as UBIT at corporate rates. Can we get around UBIT? Yes, it is possible, with the help of a tax lawyer. One of the more common methods is to invest in an offshore fund, such as one registered in Bermuda or the Cayman Islands.

A good, modestly leveraged convertible arbitrage program still has modest volatility—perhaps 10% or less per year—and a low correlation with the stock and bond markets.

Interest Rate Arbitrage

The spreads between two different interest rates vary over time. I'm refer-ring to interest rate spreads such as those between long bonds and Trea-sury bills, between corporate bonds and Treasury bonds of a similar duration, or between mortgage-backed securities (like GNMAs) and Trea-sury bonds. A manager may feel he has very little ability to predict the di-rection of interest rates (few managers do), but he may be competent at predicting the direction of certain interest rate spreads.

If so, he can capitalize on that expertise through a long/short portfolio, which is indifferent to the direction of interest rates in general. He can, for example, go long Treasuries and short mortgage-backed securities when he believes the interest rate spread is too narrow and is likely to widen, and vice versa when the spread seems too wide. Either way, he would be indif-ferent to the direction of interest rates in general.

The manager, however, doesn't make much money when he is right, nor lose much money when he is wrong. He must leverage to make the effort worthwhile. In some cases, he can invest as much as 10 times the net value of the account in a long portfolio and an equal amount in a short portfolio and still have only a relatively modest standard deviation of returns.

Leverage 10 times?! That sounds like rolling the dice—high returns or disaster, and monumental volatility! Unfortunately, the word leverage is one of those emotion-laden words that get in the way of real understanding. Un-leveraged investments—as in a start-up company—can be extremely risky, whereas a highly leveraged interest-rate arbitrage account may conceivably be less risky than a standard unleveraged bond account. The point is this: Leverage is not necessarily either good or bad. It all depends on how much leverage is used, how it is used, the underlying volatility of the leveraged in-vestment, and—of course—the expertise of the manager.

In 1999 a private sector group called the Counterparty Management Policy Group issued a report to the SEC that said, in part, "The policy group believes that leverage, while an extremely important concept with broad in-tuitive appeal, is not an independent risk factor whose measure can provide useful insights for risk managers. . . . Rather, leverage is best assessed by its effects, which can be observed in the possible amplification of market risk, funding liquidity risk and asset liquidity risk. . . . In a world of active portfo-lio management, an increase in leverage may be associated with a decrease in market risk."[4]

---

[4]Phyllis Feinberg, "Report Concludes Leverage Isn't Independent Risk Factor," *Pension & Investments*, September 6, 1999.

As we mentioned before, leverage generally leads to Unrelated Business Income Tax (UBIT). If we get over the UBIT hurdle with an interest-rate arbitrage program, we should have an account that has essentially no correlation with the ups and downs of either the stock or bond markets. Will it make money for us? Only if we have a talented manager.

Caveat

But wait a minute! What happened in September 1998 to Long-Term Capital Management, L.P., with its Nobel-prize-winning strategists? It nearly went bankrupt and probably would have if the Federal Reserve had not taken some action to generate a rescue. Long-Term Capital was perhaps the ultimate arbitrageur. Doesn't that mean that arbitrage is, in fact, an area where mortals should fear to tread?

Long-Term Capital certainly gave arbitrage a bad name. But our constructive reaction should not be to shy away from sensible arbitrage strategies but to learn from Long-Term Capital's mistakes.

Long-Term Capital adopted a strategy I have urged throughout this book to reduce risk—diversification. It scattered investments among a great many kinds of arbitrage worldwide that have low correlations with one another—low correlations over time, that is. It failed to remember that on rare occasions, when panics occur in markets worldwide, no one wants to buy anything that has even a semblance of perceived risk, and prices plummet. Correlations among arbitrage strategies that are normally very low suddenly zoom toward 1.0—as in a chain reaction.

Because natural market forces tend eventually to drive the spreads being arbitraged back to some semblance of normalcy, Long-Term Capital's strategy probably would not have been flawed if Long-Term Capital had staying power to survive the liquidity crisis. But it didn't.

Long-Term Capital had leveraged its entire $5 billion portfolio—not just well-chosen parts of it—twenty-five times! As prices fell, Long-Term Capital received margin calls—demands from its brokers to increase its security deposits. Long-Term Capital had based its strategy on the expectation that it could readily sell its holdings whenever it wished at reasonable prices. But when it went to sell, it found markets had dried up for all but the highest quality and most liquid investments. It was a time when virtually all arbitrageurs lost money—at least on paper—but they survived. Long-Term Capital, however, was forced to sell. Without an infusion of cash, Long-Term Capital would have to realize such large losses that its total liabilities threatened to exceed its total assets. That's a definition of the brink of bankruptcy.

So what's the moral to the story? We should ask our *adviser* enough questions to satisfy ourselves that the *manager* has the discipline and staying power to survive when markets suddenly become illiquid.

Managed Futures

To many investors, commodity futures[5] seem like spinning a roulette wheel. And clearly, that can be a good analogy. But it doesn't have to be.

We all too quickly associate commodity futures with pork bellies, one of the least traded commodities. There are more than 50 exchange-traded commodities worldwide, including metals, agricultural products, petroleum products, foreign currencies, and interest rate futures.

Most of those who trade commodity futures are hedgers, businesspeople who are buying insurance. The farmer sells corn futures because he can't afford the risk of fluctuating corn prices at harvest time. The importer buys futures on the Japanese yen because he can't afford unpredictable fluctuations in his cost of goods sold. Hedgers are not always in equilibrium. At times, more hedgers need to buy than to sell, or vice versa.

For commodity markets, liquidity is provided by "speculators." That's another emotion-laden word that gets in the way of real understanding. Speculators serve a valuable economic function, and the best of them are among the more quantitative academics in the investment world. They absorb the volatility in most commodity markets. They minimize their volatility by investing in a wide range of commodities with little or no correlation with one another, and they rationally expect to make a long-term profit on their investments.

The MLM Index of commodity futures, established at the beginning of 1988, provides perhaps the best evidence of how those insurance premiums get realized.

The index is totally different from a stock or bond index. As reconsti-

---

[5]An example of commodity futures would be a contract to buy an amount of corn by a specific date for $X/bushel. We can buy that future today and are betting that we will be able to sell that future later for a higher price. We certainly don't want delivery of all that corn!

tuted in December 2004, the index records the returns on a portfolio of 22 different futures, which are divided into three baskets:

- Commodities (11 futures)
- Currencies (6 futures)
- Bonds (5 futures)

These baskets are weighted by their relative historical volatility so that each will have roughly equal impact on the index. Within each basket, the futures are equal weighted. The portfolio of futures is rebalanced every 21 days under a simple mechanistic algorithm: If the current price of a future is above its average over its 252-business-day moving average, the index goes long that future; if it is below, the index goes short. The underlying cash is invested in T-bills.

Since its 1988 inception, net of hypothetical fees and expenses of nearly 2% per year, the index has provided a 7% return with a 6% volatility, and a *negative* .2 correlation with the S&P 500, and a positive .1 to .2 correlation with the Lehman Aggregate bond index.

If the index were leveraged three times, with commensurately higher expenses, its net return since 1988 would have been 13%, with an annual standard deviation of 18%, roughly the same as for common stocks—and the same slightly negative correlations as the unleveraged index, promising strong diversification benefits.

Portable Alpha

Over longer intervals, arbitrage programs offer the attraction of a very low correlation with other investments, but only the more exceptional ones can be expected to provide the same high long-term returns as a common stock account. It is nice to diversify, but I always hate to give up expected return for the privilege of diversifying.

Well, here is a place where it is possible to have our cake and eat it too—by combining an arbitrage program with an index fund (or a tactical asset allocation account) that is invested entirely through the use of index futures. We can invest in an S&P 500 index fund, for example, without buying a single stock. We can match the index with great precision either (a) by buying index futures and keeping our cash in a money-market fund or (b) by swapping cash returns plus a few basis points for S&P returns.

We can then turn the index fund into an actively managed account by, instead of investing our cash in a money market fund, putting it in any arbitrage program that has low volatility and a low correlation with the stock market. Why might we want to do that?

An exceptional manager of large common stocks, net of fees, might over the long term be able to outperform the S&P 500 by 2 percentage points a year, and a great bond manager might outperform a bond index by 1 percentage point. But if we have a low-volatility arbitrage manager who can be expected to outperform LIBOR by 3 or 4 percentage points per year (after fees), we can pair him with a manager of index futures (without either manager having to know he is so paired) and expect the index return plus 3 or 4 percentage points, or more.

Don't the combined accounts have a higher volatility than the index fund? Yes, but not much higher if the arbitrage account is really market neutral.

Incidentally, why call it Portable Alpha? Because if we let alpha stand for "excess return above our benchmark," we can synthesize a high-alpha bond or stock portfolio by investing in an arbitrage account (the source of the alpha) and overlaying that account with index futures (the benchmark). We transport the arbitrageur's alpha to a stock or bond account. We can mix and match as we please with Portable Alphas.

Portable Alphas are not yet widely used by taxfree funds—perhaps because they are complex, offbeat, and difficult for committee members to grasp. That leaves all the more opportunity to those taxfree funds that are enterprising and willing to open their minds.

Hedge Funds

The arbitrage programs described above are often included under the term "hedge funds." The Commonfund Benchmark Study includes them as "hedge funds" when it shows that 28% of endowment funds of all sizes invest in hedge funds.

But here I will use the term "hedge funds" to denote funds other than those intended to be market neutral, to denote funds that are generally more long than short. Even so, the term "hedge funds" covers a wide range of investment approaches. Virtually all hedge funds sell stocks short as well as have a normal "long" portfolio. That is where commonality ends. Some are quite conservative. Others are highly leveraged to the markets. Most invest mainly in stocks; others invest in the gamut of assets, including many derivatives.

Most share one thing in common—high fees, often a fixed fee equal to

1% of asset values each year plus 20% of all net profits. We should not be surprised that many of the very best investment managers become hedge fund managers, because their compensation can be astronomical. And if the manager is good enough, the high fees can be worth our paying. After all, the only thing that counts for the investor is long-term returns net of fees, and certain hedge funds have provided some of the best returns available.

The problem is that the high fees of a hedge fund don't necessarily mean high returns. There have been well-publicized instances of investors' value in a hedge fund being completely wiped out by the manager's speculation. We therefore must have extraordinary confidence in a hedge fund manager in order to agree to his high fees.

Another drawback of hedge funds is that they have not usually been very forthcoming about the composition of their portfolios. Institutional investors may find it difficult to plug the composition of hedge funds into their fund's overall asset allocation. Transparency has improved in recent years, however, under continuing pressure from investors.

It is true that some of the best investment managers of our time are hedge fund managers, and they have made their investors rich. Is our *adviser* up to identifying who they are?

One way to approach such hedge funds (or market neutral funds) is through a fund of funds. Yes, that adds another heavy layer of fees. But the fees may be worth it if the fund of funds (a) has long experience in identifying the best funds, (b) is investing in many hedge funds that are closed to new investors (because wise hedge fund managers recognize that size can limit their returns and therefore their incentive fees), and (c) has a competent staff to follow closely all of the funds in its portfolio.

ILLIQUID INVESTMENTS

Illiquid investments are private investments that may be difficult to sell within a year, or perhaps impossible to get out of for the next 5, 10, or 15 years. Illiquid investments—usually limited partnerships—include:

- Real estate funds
- Venture capital funds
- Other private corporate investments, such as buy-in or buy-out funds
- Distressed securities (most of which are illiquid)
- Timberland funds
- Oil and gas properties

Characteristics of Illiquidity

Are illiquid investments prudent? Yes, provided we have enough marketable securities that we can convert to cash in time to meet our *fund's* potential payout requirements.

Most *investment funds* hold far more liquid assets than they need, and by doing so, they may be incurring a material opportunity cost. As a general rule, the more marketable an asset, the higher its price is bid up, and therefore the lower the return we can expect from it. That's why prices of the largest, most active stocks generally carry a "liquidity premium" over prices of less actively traded stocks. We pay a price for liquidity.

Conversely, prices of illiquid investments should be lower. There should be an "illiquidity premium" to the net return on private, illiquid investments. The word "premium" is in quotes because caveat emptor applies especially to private, illiquid investments, which come with fees far higher than fees on normal common stock accounts. But if we can invest intelligently in a diversified group of private, illiquid investments, we should expect a somewhat higher return per unit of risk than on marketable securities.

"Active managers willing to accept illiquidity achieve a significant edge in seeking high risk-adjusted returns," writes David Swensen of the Yale endowment fund. "Because market players routinely overpay for liquidity, serious investors benefit by avoiding overpriced liquid securities and locating bargains in less widely followed, less liquid market segments."[6]

Because of the difficulties of valuing private investments, and because a private investment purchases its assets over time and then sells them over time, time-weighted rates of return have little meaning. We should evaluate the performance of a private investment by dollar-weighted rates of return (internal rates of return, or IRR). And again, because valuations are so suspect, the only solid performance figure of a private investment is its dollar-weighted rate of return on our contributions, calculated from our first contribution to the last payout we receive—net of all fees and expenses, of course.

Caveats

Because private investments funds are illiquid, our *investment fund* should hold only a small percentage of its assets in any one private investment

---

[6]David F. Swensen, *Pioneering Portfolio Management* (The Free Press, 2000), p. 56.

fund. If we would like a meaningful allocation to private investments, we should build a portfolio of diverse private investments funds over time. We want diversification by kind and by time. Time diversification is important in private investments because there are common factors that impact returns to partnerships of each vintage year, and it is close to impossible to divine up front which vintage year's partnerships will be most successful.

If we are a small endowment fund, say, less than $50 or $100 million in assets, we might be better off sticking with liquid assets. If we do go into private investments, we would probably want to use a fund of funds, which can give us instant diversification. But, of course, the fund of funds charges a high fee on top of the high fees charged by sponsors of private investment funds.

Also, it is even more important than with marketable securities to be with the very best. Median returns of private investment funds have not been very attractive. This is best illustrated by the long-term results of venture capital funds, where there is a wide difference in performance between the better and the poorer funds. Among venture capital partnerships started between 1980 and 1995, the difference in IRR between the first-quartile performer and the median was nearly 9 percentage points per year, and between median and the third-quartile performer, some 8 percentage points per year.[7] Those are humongous differences, especially when we consider that 25% did better than first quartile and 25% were lower than third quartile.

Perhaps the leading manager of funds of venture capital funds, whose every fund from its first in 1985 has had first-quartile returns, achieved a net IRR of 29% over the 19 years through 2003. By comparison, the median venture capital fund returned only 9%, which means that half the venture capital funds returned 9% or less. Investors in the majority of venture capital funds could not have felt well rewarded![8]

PRIVATE ASSET CLASSES

Real Estate

Of all private, illiquid investments, real estate funds are the asset class most widely used. Real estate is truly a major asset class, since close to half of

---

[7]Per *Venture Economics*, IRR's are through year-end 1999.
[8]Ibid.

the world's wealth may lie in real estate. Moreover, real estate values have had a relatively modest correlation with those of stocks and bonds, making real estate a useful diversifier. Even if our portfolio includes REITs among its liquid asset classes, private real estate funds may be worth considering as well.

Real estate is often viewed as an inflation hedge. While far from perfect, I believe real estate is a better long-term inflation hedge than most other asset classes. Few asset classes have investment returns more highly correlated with inflation.

As always, diversification counts, and it's helpful to diversify real estate:

1. *By type.* Mainly office (downtown and suburban), retail (major malls and strip centers), industrial parks (warehouses and light industrial), apartments, and perhaps single family residential, hotels, and raw land.

2. *Geographically.* The various parts of the country, such as Northeast, Southeast, Midwest, Southwest, Mountain States, and Pacific. (For this purpose, the United States is often divided into economic zones that have the lowest correlations with one another.)

3. *By size of property.* Such as properties valued at less than $15 million, those between $15 and $75 million, and those valued at more than $75 million.

Diversification is advantageous because it lowers the volatility of our real estate portfolio. For example, offices in one area may get overbuilt, with values thereby declining, while apartment vacancies may fall unusually low in another area, resulting in premium rents and prices for apartments there. These individual cycles are additional, of course, to the overall cycles in commercial real estate.

What rates of return can one expect from core real estate—from properties purchased with the intention of holding them for the long term? The NCREIF index (National Council of Real Estate Investment Fiduciaries) is the best index of U.S. commercial real estate returns available. It shows that over the 20 years ending in 2003 aggregate net total returns (if we assume about 1% per year in management fees) were just over $6^1/_2$% per year (about $3^1/_2$% real returns, net of inflation), with a standard deviation of $3^1/_2$% per year and a correlation with the S&P 500 of about zero. Given these figures, what should we expect of real estate?

The above return figures include the years of 1989–1993 when commercial real estate went through its worst depression since the 1930s. I expect that real returns in a more normal interval would be higher than the $3^1/_2\%$. For that 1982–2003 interval real estate returns were $6^1/_2$ percentage points per year lower than those of the S&P 500. While that difference should narrow dramatically, I still don't believe long term we can expect quite as high returns from core real estate as from common stocks.

Volatility of real estate is not nearly as low as the $3^1/_2\%$ NCREIF figure. This reflects the fact that appraisals mask much volatility in the real estate market. Even so, I believe volatility is lower than for common stocks.

The one figure I largely believe is the correlation with the S&P 500 of essentially zero. Although private real estate and common stocks are both impacted by economic factors, they are impacted by different factors and at different times. While the stock market was enjoying an historic boom during the decade 1989–1998, returning over 19% per year, private real estate barely scratched out 5% per year. Then real estate did relatively well during the stock market debacle of 2000–2002. A key advantage of real estate is that it is a good portfolio diversifier.

Venture Real Estate   An approach to real estate investing that I like better—especially if we also invest in REITs—is what I call "venture real estate." Simplistically, it's where a manager buys a property to which he can add material value (as through construction or rehabilitation), then adds that value in a timely manner and promptly sells the property to someone who wants to buy some good core real estate.

The approach is far more management-intensive than core real estate and requires greater expertise. That's why I refer to it as venture real estate.

If we pursue this approach, we should be sure we have especially competent managers, and we should target net investment returns that are higher than those on common stocks—at least 8% real (in excess of inflation). In fact, I prefer to wait until we find exceptional real estate funds from which we can expect net IRRs of at least 10% to 12% real, or 15% nominal, and then invest in a diversity of such funds.

Individually, venture real estate projects may be more volatile than core real estate, but it is possible, through commingled funds, to build a highly diversified portfolio of venture real estate. I am not convinced that such a diversified venture portfolio is materially more volatile than core real estate. Nor do I think the correlation with common stock returns is any higher. I believe there is a higher degree of "diversifiable risk" in venture real estate (as opposed to "systematic risk," which cannot be diversified away).

The best approach for investing in private real estate is, in my opinion, commingled funds, since they can provide immediate diversification. The challenge is to find the best-managed commingled funds and then to negotiate a partnership agreement that aligns the financial motivations of the manager with those of the investors.

In-House Management of Real Estate   Some of the larger *investment funds* invest in their our own portfolio of properties. They thereby retain maximum control. They themselves decide which properties to buy, how to manage them, whether to leverage them, and when to sell. And they may avoid the substantial fees that are built into commingled funds and REITs.

Drawbacks are that managing such a portfolio takes a lot of real estate expertise and time on the part of staff or an outside adviser, and it is difficult to get as broad portfolio diversification.

Venture Capital

According to the Commonfund study, nearly a quarter of all endowment funds larger than $50 million invest in venture capital.

There are broad and narrow definitions of venture capital, and here we'll use a narrow definition: investment in private start-up companies, mostly high-tech companies. These companies may be as early-stage as an idea and a business plan, or as late-stage as a private company that is already producing a product, needs expansion capital, and may be preparing to go public (make an initial public offering of its stock). As thus defined, venture capital is probably the riskiest of investments. Most start-up companies fail to survive, and only a small percentage become highly successful. How can our fund invest prudently in such risky ventures?

Fortunately, there has developed in the United States the world's most effective environment for funding and nurturing start-up businesses. Its venture capital industry is one of the United States' real competitive advantages. A key to this process, and one that provides a sensible way to invest prudently in start-up businesses, has been the development of sophisticated venture capital investment firms.

A venture capital investment firm consists of a small group of experienced people who have become expert at evaluating start-up enterprises, identifying the most promising, investing in the best of them, taking seats on their boards, putting them in touch with those who can provide expertise they happen to need, and advising them on business strategy and raising capital. These venture capital firms form limited partnerships and raise funds from wealthy persons and institutional investors.

Each partnership may invest its capital over three to five years in some 25 different startup companies, and the fund may take some 15 to 20 years before it is able to convert the last of its investments into cash through either acquisition or an initial public offering (IPO)—or must write them off through bankruptcy.

Despite its manager's expert winnowing and nurturing, many ventures are losers. Most of the rest earn only a modest rate of return. A few home runs make or break the fund. To illustrate, one of the best managers of funds of venture capital funds invested indirectly in 2,637 different ventures between 1985 and 2001. Just 25 home runs—less than 1% of those ventures—provided 43% of all returns, and the 8% that repaid at least 10 times their cost provided 72% of all returns. Yet these would be above average results.

Venture capital investing is very labor-intensive, and the fees charged by such venture capital partnerships are very high—typically $2\frac{1}{2}\%$ per year of an investor's commitment to the fund, plus 20% of cumulative net profits.

Net internal rates of return (IRRs) to the investors over the life of a venture capital partnership range from –10% per year to +40%, and in some cases more extreme. That's a far narrower range than for individual start-up companies, but it's still an extraordinarily wide range of results from an investment with an average duration of seven or eight years.

The task for us investors is to diversify among the best venture capital partnerships or enter a fund of venture capital funds, then dollar-average into additional partnerships over time in order to reduce the range of our aggregate net IRR expectations. Time diversification is very important in venture capital because there are common factors that impact returns to partnerships of each vintage year, and it is close to impossible to divine up front which vintage year's partnerships will be most successful.

The median venture capital partnership started in the 1980s provided a disappointing return, while the median partnership begun in 1990–1995 achieved nearly 23%, and those that started in the next few years earned far higher. Then in 1999–2000 nearly three times as many venture-backed companies were formed as in 1995–1997.[9] This number declined to a low

---

[9]Ibid.

level by 2002, but returns on the companies formed during that bubble have been disappointing.

Well diversified, a good venture capital partnership should earn a net long-term IRR of 15% to 20%—well worth an allocation of several percent of our assets. But these returns come in a lumpy fashion, and most partnerships have negative or flat returns in their first few years, as fees are greater than returns.

Buy-In Funds

Buy-in funds (like venture capital funds) also invest in private companies, but companies that are more established, usually ones that are or have been profitable. Such companies need capital for expansion, for acquisitions, or perhaps even for turn-around. The fund buys privately issued common stock or convertible securities or a combination of bonds and warrants.[10]

Abroad, both buy-in and buy-out funds are usually referred to as venture capital funds, but few invest in start-up companies.

The risk of investing in a going concern is clearly less than investing in a start-up company, but the opportunity to earn 10 or 20 times our investment is also much lower.

Investors pay fees to the manager of the buy-in fund that in total, including performance fees, are much higher than for a typical common stock program. Hence, the investor should demand a premium return because of both illiquidity and increased risk. The investor should be highly convinced that, net of all costs, he can realistically expect to earn that premium return.

Whenever the buy-in fund makes an investment, it should have an exit plan—a process and time line for getting its money out, often through an assurance that a public stock offering can be held by a given date, or a promise that the company will be willing to buy back the securities at a certain price by a certain date (a put).

Buy-Out Funds and LBOs

A buy-out fund purchases the whole company instead of simply providing a portion of the company's capital. In the process, it either gives strong

---

[10]Warrants are options to buy stock at a certain price up to a certain date.

support to the existing management team or installs new senior management. In either case, it usually ensures management's sharp focus by providing lucrative stock options to the senior executives.

Sometimes, mainly in the United States, the company is acquired chiefly with debt—in what is known as a leveraged buy-out (LBO). LBO funds typically finance some 60% or more of an acquisition's purchase price with debt. The strategy takes advantage of the fact that interest on debt is tax deductible, which sharply reduces the income tax bill previously faced by the company. (Without the advantage of tax deductibility of interest on debt, I doubt that there would be such a thing as LBOs. There would be buyouts, but not *leveraged* buyouts.) An LBO leverages the investment for the relatively small number of outstanding common shares. Hence, if the company is moderately successful, the share owners can realize internal rates of return above 50% and possibly above 100%.

Such leverage also incurs high risk, of course. A modest decline in the company's fortunes can leave it unable to meet its debt obligations and thereby lead to bankruptcy. In that case, the common stock investors (and sometimes the high-yield bond investors as well) may lose their entire investment.

Hence, a very high premium is placed on the competency of the management of the buy-out fund in its selection of appropriate companies to buy and in its ability to install excellent management in the companies once it buys them.

Distressed Securities

Another alternative asset class consists of the vultures of the investment world—distressed security funds. Just as vultures contribute to the ecology by cleaning up the carrion, distressed security funds buy loans or securities that other investors no longer want.

When a company heads toward bankruptcy, many investors want out. Helping a company avoid bankruptcy or nursing it through bankruptcy is a particular skill that many investors do not have. The skill involves specialized legal expertise combined with negotiating strategies and corporate management skills that are a far cry from those required of normal stock and bond investors.

There are basically two kinds of distressed investors: (1) One will try to become part of the bankruptcy proceedings and thereby influence the outcome. Such an investor may try to obtain as many of the outstanding shares or loans as possible so he can control the vote on any issues before the court. (2) Other distressed investors avoid becoming part of the bank-ruptcy proceedings, partly because of the process's heavy demands on their time and expense, but more often in order to retain flexibility. Such an in-vestor can sell at any time, while one involved with the bankruptcy court becomes an insider and, in effect, has his investment locked up until the court's final resolution.

The proliferation of LBOs and high-yield bonds in recent years promises to provide a continuing supply of distressed securities, as a cer-tain portion of these investments will predictably get into trouble. Well-managed distressed security funds can provide good returns and useful diversification to our portfolio.

Timberland

For the patient investor, timber offers outstanding diversification benefits and the prospect of moderately high long-term returns. Timber is one of the better inflation hedges, and its returns have had a very low correlation with those of stocks and bonds. Forecasts of net long-term real rates of re-turn (net of inflation) from timberland range upwards from 6%.

Patience is necessary because of the cyclicality of timber values and be-cause active management of timberland takes years to pay off. But depend-ing on the price of timberland, the case for timber is fairly persuasive:

- Despite the use of wood substitutes and the impact of electronic com-munications on the printed page, the demand for timber should con-tinue to increase in the years ahead, especially as living standards rise in the developing countries of the world.

- Increasingly, timber will have to come from timber farms, because nat-ural forests have been cut so heavily, and remaining natural forests are gaining more and more environmental protection.

- The percentage of the world's timber that today is provided from tim-ber farms is very small. As demand continues to rise, supply is likely to be constrained. Creating a new timber farm that is ready to harvest takes at least 20 years.

- We're not likely to be surprised by a sudden increase in the supply of timber, as the supply for the next 15 to 20 years is pretty well known. It's already in the ground and growing.

- Timber is a commodity that does not have to be harvested at any one time. Each year, a tree continues to grow, and it becomes more valuable per cubic foot until it reaches some 30 years of age (depending on the kind of tree). Such in-growth amounts to 6% to 8% per year.

- Some of the best places for growing timber are in the southern hemisphere, such as New Zealand, Australia, Chile, Brazil, and South Africa. Many trees will grow twice as fast there as in the United States, where in turn, trees grow faster than in Canada or northern Europe.
- Over the past century, the real price of timber (net of inflation) has fluctuated a great deal, but overall it has risen by some 1% per year.

Investments in timberland programs are long-term investments, but unless liquidity is particularly important to our fund (it normally shouldn't be), a few percent of our portfolio in timberland seems to make a lot of sense—especially if spread over a range of investment years.

Oil and Gas Properties

Oil and gas properties are a volatile but diversifying investment for a taxfree fund. They offer better inflation protection than most asset classes, and their returns have had a meaningfully negative correlation with returns on stocks and bonds. They also provide strong cash flow.

Returns on oil and gas properties are highly dependent on energy prices, which have deep cycles that can last for decades. They are also impacted, but to a lesser extent, by the accuracy of estimates of a well's reserves.

Because of the uncertainty of energy prices, oil and gas properties are usually priced to provide double digit real returns, assuming the real (inflation-adjusted) price of oil and gas doesn't change. During the 1980s and the first half of he 1990s, double digit real returns (or even nominal returns) were a pipe dream, as a result of weak energy prices. During the 1970s, however, oil and gas properties were the place to be.

Participations can be bought in producing wells, development drilling, and exploratory drilling. Other oil and gas investments encompass the gamut of oil service companies—from drilling supplies to pipelines to gas storage salt mines—and these can be effective and diversifying investments in a private energy portfolio.

The costs of investing in oil and gas, including hidden costs, can be high. And we must invest in such a way as not to be an oil and gas operator, or else our taxfree fund will be subject to Unrelated Business Income Tax. Every time I have ventured into the oil patch, I have felt a bit like the city slicker waiting to be fleeced. In short, I want an extremely competent and reliable manager who really knows his way around the oil patch. If we have such a manager, however, we should find it worthwhile long-term to invest several percent of our total assets in oil and gas properties.

IN SHORT

- Alternative investments—anything other than marketable stocks, bonds, and cash—can add valuable diversification to our portfolio. More and more *investment funds* are allocating a growing portion of their assets to these investments.
- Because these asset classes are especially dependent on the skill of the investment manager, we need to invest with only the best managers.
- This chapter is included as a reference, so we can recognize these asset classes if our *adviser* should raise some of them for discussion.

CHAPTER 6

Selecting and Monitoring Investment Managers

Once we have developed our *fund's* objectives and its Policy Asset Allocation, we must decide who will manage the investments in each asset class.

What should be our overriding goal? We should strive to obtain the best possible *managers* in each individual asset class—the *managers* who are most likely to produce the best future performance.

Such perfection is obviously unattainable. No one can realistically evaluate all *managers* in the world. And simply chasing *managers* with the best track record is a losing game, because all *managers* have hot and cold streaks. Also, some of the best *managers* won't accept our money. Finally, no one can come even close to being a perfect judge of the future performance of an *investment manager*. But the best possible *managers* should still be our goal.

That goal implies:

- No constraints or preferences as to geography or kind of manager (small, large, here, there, bank, independent firm, etc.).
- A commitment to objectivity. That does not mean relying only on numbers and ascertainable facts. Ultimately, these decisions come down to judgments. But we should make decisions as dispassionately as possible.

THREE BASIC APPROACHES

There are three basic ways for an *investment fund* to go about investing:

1. Index funds
2. In-house (do-it-ourselves)
3. Outside managers

Index Funds

For stocks or bonds, an index fund should not only be our benchmark. It should also be our investment vehicle of choice unless we can find a *manager* in that asset class who we are confident will do better—net of all fees and expenses. The case for index funds is persuasively articulated by Jack Bogle in *Common Sense on Mutual Funds* (John Wiley & Sons, Inc., 1999).

Let's consider the Wilshire 5000 index initially. This is a capitalization-weighted index of all stocks traded in the United States. It is a truism that the average active investor has to underperform the Wilshire 5000 in his U.S. investments. The investor has trading costs and investment management fees that in combination can equal 0.5% to 1.5% per year, whereas we can invest in an index fund that closely matches the Wilshire 5000 index with minimum cost.[1] So the odds are against active investing.

The most widely used index fund is one that replicates Standard & Poor's 500 index, which is very heavily weighted toward the largest U.S. stocks and has a growth-stock bias. These are widely researched stocks. It is difficult for any investor to get an information advantage over other investors in large U.S. stocks. As a result, the pricing of large U.S. stocks is often thought to be very efficient. That means that if a good active investor stays within the S&P 500 stock universe, it is difficult for him to produce net returns that outperform that index over the long term. If we choose an active *manager* over an index fund for these stocks, we must be arrogant about our ability to choose active *managers*—and then we must prove our right to be arrogant.

As we consider active managers, we should be aware of the fact that most active managers not only should underperform the broad indexes theoretically but also have underperformed:

- "In the 25 years ending with 1997, on a cumulative basis, over three-quarters of professionally managed funds underperformed the S&P 500," according to Charlie Ellis of Greenwich Research Associates.[2]
- In the year 2000, "data from *Morningstar* show that of 5,253 domestic, non-index, equity mutual funds, 769 have performance records of

---

[1]The Vanguard 500 Index fund has an expense ratio of 0.18%, and with enough size, the cost of an S&P 500 index fund can get as low as 0.01%.
[2]Charles Ellis, *Winning the Loser's Game: Timeless Strategies for Successful Investing* (McGraw-Hill Professional Publishing, 1998).

10 years or more. Of these 769 funds, only 195 [25%] have generated annualized returns greater than that of the Wilshire 5000 index over the past 10 years, after accounting for the impact of fees and sales loads," according to Mark Armbruster of WealthCFO.

Is an S&P 500 index fund therefore a no-brainer? Well, intuitively, does it make a lot of sense to increase the weighting of a stock in our portfolio as its price goes up, and vice versa (as an index fund implicitly does)? That would make sense if the change in this year's price is a good predictor of next year's price, but we know that isn't true. In fact, contrarian investors have long known that a pervasive general trend in the investment world is reversion to the mean.[3]

The active investor has another advantage: He is able to invest outside the index that is used for his benchmark. For instance, from a practical standpoint, a large-stock investor may be able to invest in a 700-stock universe—not just the 500 stocks included in the S&P 500. In fact, most active investors periodically do go outside their benchmark universe. That is undoubtedly why active investors as a group will outperform the S&P 500 for a period of years, and then underperform it for another period of years.

We've been talking mainly about large stocks. One can also invest in a smaller stock index fund such as a Russell 2000 index fund in the U.S. Would that make just as much sense?

Because smaller stocks are not as widely researched, it is possible for a good investor who digs hard enough to gain an information advantage on other investors and therefore outperform a small-stock index by a wider margin than a good large-stock investor can outperform the S&P 500. But if the opportunity is greater with small stocks, the reverse is true as well. One can really get bagged with small stocks. In short, if we are careful in

---

[3]"Reversion to the mean" is the tendency for the price of an asset (or an asset class) that has greatly outperformed or underperformed the average of other assets (or asset classes) to revert over time toward the average. That tendency, which in general has been well documented, also makes some intuitive sense.

For example, if a company is earning a particularly high rate of return in a line of business, its high earnings will attract competitors to that line of business. The competitors will challenge the pricing flexibility of the company and limit its subsequent returns. Conversely, a company that is performing poorly attracts takeover bids from other managements who believe they can squeeze more value out of the company.

selecting *managers*, I believe for most *investment funds* active management of small stocks can make more sense than a Russell 2000 index fund.

Viable index funds are available for large stocks in all the developed countries. Since there are so many countries with different dynamics, it would intuitively seem that an active investor should be able to add a lot of value through country allocation alone. But that hasn't proved easy to do—unless the *manager* was smart (or lucky) enough to underweight Japanese stocks starting in 1990, and to fully weight them in the 1980s, when at one point Japanese stocks accounted for more than 60% of the non-U.S. index.

Reliable index funds for investment-grade U.S. bonds are also available and compete very well with active bond *managers*. In selecting an active fixed income *manager*, it is equally important to ask ourselves—do we really have sound reason to believe that, net of fees and expenses, this *manager* can meaningfully outperform an index fund? In short, index funds are a very viable bond alternative. Yes, it is entirely possible to do better, but how much better?

Returns in excess of an index fund—always hard to achieve—have been more readily achievable in some asset classes than in others. In small stocks, U.S. or non-U.S., and in emerging markets stocks, first quartile managers were able to add alpha of more than 3% per year during the 10 years ending in mid-2000. Meanwhile, in large U.S. growth stocks first quartile managers were able to add less than 1%/year and in high-grade bonds less than 0.5% per year.[4]

In-House Management

Index funds can be managed inexpensively in-house, but fees are so low for outside-managed index funds, it is hard to justify in-house management. Hence, in our discussion of in-house management, we shall focus on active management.

Many sponsors of large *investment funds* actively manage all or a portion of their assets in-house. They avoid the high fees charged by active managers by hiring a staff to buy and sell the assets themselves. If we are large enough, is this the way to go?

Let's go back to our original goal—to have the best possible *managers* in each asset class. With respect to whatever asset class we are talk-

---

[4]*Source:* BARRA RogersCasey.

ing about, can we objectively convince ourselves that *we* can put together a management team that, net of all costs, can match or exceed the net results of the best *managers* we could hire outside? If so, then in-house is the way to go.

In-house management, however, faces serious challenges. For example, does our compensation schedule enable us to attract some of the best possible investment managers? And if we hire some smart young people and are lucky enough to grow them into the best, can we keep them? The best managers tend to be entrepreneurial people who want ownership in their own firm. Even if we insulate our investment management team from the rest of our bureaucratic organization, can we realistically aspire to hire and retain the best?

And if our in-house hires don't ultimately challenge the best we can hire outside, we have the unpleasant task of putting them out on the street. That's a lot tougher than terminating an outside *manager*.

Outside Managers

In each individual asset class we should seek the best *manager* (or *managers*) we can get, regardless of geographic location. With literally thousands of *managers* to choose from, our *adviser* should recommend ones for each asset class. What kind of questions should we ask about those recommendations? Why does the *adviser* believe his candidate is the best we can get in that asset class? And how does the candidate meet our criteria for the hiring and retention of *managers*?

CRITERIA FOR HIRING AND RETAINING MANAGERS

Our criteria should be the same for both new and existing *managers*:

1. **Character.** Integrity and reliability. Can we give this *manager* our wholehearted trust?
2. **Investment approach.** Do the assumptions and principles underlying the *manager's* approach make sense to us?
3. **Expected return.** The *manager's* historic return, net of fees, overlaid by an evaluation of the predictive value of that historic return, as well as other factors that may seem relevant in that instance and may have predictive value.

4. **Expected impact on the *fund's* overall volatility.** Two facets:

   a. **Expected volatility**—the historic volatility of the *manager's* investments overlaid by an evaluation of the predictive value of that historic volatility, as well as a recognition of the historic volatility of that *manager's* asset class in general.

   b. **Expected correlation** of the *manager's* volatility with the rest of our portfolio.

5. **Liquidity.** How readily in the future can the account be converted to cash, and how satisfactory is that in relation to the *fund's* projected needs for cash?

6. **Control.** Can our organization, with the help of our *adviser*, adequately monitor this *investment manager* and its investment program?

7. **Legal.** Have all legal concerns been dealt with satisfactorily?

A common mistake is to be mesmerized by great past performance, without looking further. In a study of 613 U.S. common stock managers, BARRA RogersCasey found little predictive value in their performance during the five years 1991–1995 for the ensuing five years 1996–2000 (see Table 6.1). Moreover, BARRA RogersCasey found similarly discouraging predictive value in five-year returns for prior intervals.

It is crucial to focus on predictive value. What do we mean by "predictive value of historic returns?" The whole selection process has to do with predicting future performance. Past performance is irrelevant except as it may have predictive value. What's done is done. The only thing we can im-

TABLE 6.1   Study of the Predictive Value of Past Performance

	Subsequent 5-Year Results for 1st Quartile Performers during the 5 years 1991–95		Subsequent 5-Year Results for 4th Quartile Performers during the 5 years 1991–95	
	1st Quartile	4th Quartile	1st Quartile	4th Quartile
Large value	24%	32%	30%	16%
Large growth	37	22	20	34
Core large cap	38	31	20	33
Small value	23	23	45	27
Small growth	29	24	35	15

Source: BARRA RogersCasey.

pact is the future. Hence, the future should be the exclusive focus of our investment committee.

How can we judge the predictive value of a *manager's* performance? It's not easy, and in each case it comes down to a judgment on which reasonable people who have studied all the facts may differ. My judgment has tended to be influenced by the following factors:

- **Decision makers.** Who is the individual or individuals responsible for the performance record (they may not necessarily be the heads of the firm)? Have the same individuals been responsible throughout? If so, are they still in the saddle? If not, predictive value is essentially nil, because the past performance reflects somebody else's work. Of all considerations, this is probably the most important.

  "Investors seeking to engage an active manager should focus on 'people, people, people.' Nothing matters more than working with high-quality partners," writes David Swensen of the Yale endowment fund.[5]

- **Support staff.** Material turnover in the research or other support staff may impair the predictive value of past performance.

- **Process.** In investment approaches where the investment process is as important as the individual decision makers—a rarity, in my judgment—I may attribute some predictive value to past performance even though there has been turnover in key people. Continuity of methodology is particularly important with quantitative *managers*—where the product of human judgment is the mathematical algorithm[6] rather than individual investment decisions. With such *managers*, I am also interested in their commitment to continuing research.

- **Size of assets managed.** If, adjusted for the growth in market capitalization of the overall stock market, a *manager* is managing a much larger value of assets today than he did X years ago, his performance of X years ago may carry very little predictive value. Managing $5 to $50 million would seem to have little predictive value for a *manager* who is now managing over $5 billion.

---

[5]David F. Swensen, *Pioneering Portfolio Management* (The Free Press, 2000), p. 252.
[6]These algorithms are mathematical equations that transform raw data about companies and the economy into specific buy and sell decisions.

- **Number of decisions.** Performance that is the result of a thousand small decisions should have a much higher predictive value than performance dominated by only a handful of decisions, as might be the case with a *manager* whose past performance hinges on several key market-timing calls. The smaller the number of data points, the more difficult it is to distinguish skill from luck.
- **Consistency.** Performance that is consistently strong relative to a valid benchmark would seem to have a lot more predictive value than performance that is all over the place.
- **Proper benchmark.** Is the *manager* being evaluated against the proper benchmark? Performance that is compared with a valid, tight-fitting benchmark would seem to have higher predictive value than performance that is simply compared with the market in general, especially over intervals as short as three to five years. Comparisons with the market in general can lead us astray, since the dominant influence may be a *manager's* style (which can go in and out of vogue) rather than the manager's skill. It may be useful to review pages 44–45 and 48 with respect to benchmarks.
- **Time.** In this case, how many years of a *manager's* past performance do we think have predictive value? Three years of performance may reflect mainly noise. I am particularly impressed when I see a *manager* with 15 years of strong performance that also meet other criteria of good predictive value.

Some quantitative *managers* who don't have long track records will show extensive simulations of how they would have performed if they had been using their quantitative method. Beware! Let's understand how the *manager* developed his algorithm in order to evaluate how much data-mining[7] the *manager* has done. It's almost impossible to eliminate data-mining completely, but let's make a hard judgment about how academically honest and objective the *manager* has been. Then, if he passes both these tests, let's discount his results by several percentage points per year and see if the *manager* is still worth considering.

Assessing the predictive value of a *manager's* past performance is not easy. But it's crucial. Assessing the likely impact of the *manager's* volatility

---

[7]Data-mining is the extent to which 20/20 hindsight has influenced the manager's algorithm.

and correlation on the rest of our portfolio is likewise not easy, but it's also important. An understanding of the volatility and correlation of the *manager's* particular asset class can be helpful, too.

Managers of Illiquid Assets We need to devote extra care to the selection of managers of the private, illiquid funds we enter. Because there is such a wide dispersion of returns between the better managers and the average managers of private funds, there is extra pressure for us to go only with the best.

The criteria for selecting managers of private investments are the same as discussed above, but evaluating the predictive value of track records is more difficult because (a) track records are often short; (b) track records are often incomplete, because typically many assets have not yet been sold; and (c) the track record often comprises a relatively small number of investments. These factors increase the challenge of selecting managers of private investments and accentuate the importance of focusing on people, people, people.

HIRING MANAGERS

Evaluating Candidates

A common way for a committee to select a *manager* is for the recommender to bring three or more candidates to meet with the committee, at the conclusion of which the committee is to select one of them. This is what I call the "beauty contest." In a 20- to 30-minute presentation, committee members are able to discern which presenter is the most articulate, but I've found little correlation between articulateness and good investing.

That's why I believe the "beauty contest" is a poor approach. Those who have participated in the full, painstaking evaluation of all the *managers* being considered are the ones best equipped to conclude who should be hired. Committee members who spend only a relatively few hours per year on our fund's investments can't hope to make a meaningful evaluation on the basis of a 20- or 30-minute presentation.

Should the *adviser* give the committee a presentation on the three best *managers* in a given asset class and then let the committee choose? I don't even favor that approach. The recommender has done the research. He should make a single recommendation and be charged with the accountability.

What, then, should I as a committee member do? Be a rubber stamp? No. I should understand the above criteria, consider whether the recommender has covered them all adequately in his presentation, and ask questions until I am satisfied. If I can't get comfortable based on the above criteria, I should try to table the recommendation or vote against it.

But remember: We committee members can't do a good job of asset allocation and *manager* selection by ourselves. The committee should probably approve of 95% of the recommendations of its *adviser* or else terminate the *adviser* and hire a new one in whom the committee does have confidence.

Caveat about Style

It is helpful initially to categorize *managers* by style. For example, common categories of styles of U.S. equity *managers* are large, medium, or small cap, and growth or value. But these style categories can only be very gross. There are great differences of style among large-cap value *managers* and among small-cap growth managers, for example. And stocks that might be considered growth stocks today may, after their bubble has burst, be considered value stocks tomorrow.

When looking at a large-cap value *manager*, which benchmark should we choose? Several value indexes are available. Any particular benchmark may relate to the *manager's* style in only a very coarse way. Where the benchmark doesn't fit very well, we should not downgrade the *manager* because of benchmark risk.[8] Many of the best *managers* don't manage to a benchmark, and shouldn't. That means we just have to work a little harder to understand and interpret their performance. Still, in the end, we want a *manager* that can—over the long term—materially outperform his benchmark net of fees.

Benchmark Risk

The more valid a benchmark is for a particular *manager*, and the more he invests within the universe of that benchmark, the narrower his deviations from that benchmark—and superficially, at least—the easier it is for us to evaluate his performance. We should never, however, confuse benchmark

---

[8]"Benchmark risk" is the risk that the *manager's* performance will deviate greatly (up and down) from his benchmark.

risk with absolute risk, or forget that our objective is to make money. A *manager* with a large benchmark risk could possibly have lower volatility than the benchmark.

Peter L. Bernstein, well-known consultant and financial writer, claims institutional investors have handcuffed their *managers* by linking them to benchmarks whose composition changes every year.[9]

David Fisher, chairman of the world-class Capital Guardian Trust Company, has succinctly placed benchmark risk in its proper context with these remarks:

- Risk management is a great deal more than benchmark risk.
- Put another way—benchmark risk is a small part of risk management.
- Organizations should be aware of benchmark risk but not pray at its altar.
- Nowhere is it written that criteria that are quantifiable are more important than those that are not.

Many investment managers are fearful of taking a lot of benchmark risk because of business risk—*their* business risk that if they should ever underperform their benchmark by a wide margin many clients would leave them. That's an understandable concern and needs to be dealt with.

One time while visiting a Canadian investment manager, we noted that he had some 20% of his portfolio in a single stock—Nortel. I asked him if he had that large an allocation because he thought Nortel was by far the most attractive stock in Canada. He replied no, he was actually far underweighted in Nortel, as that stock composed as much as 35% of his benchmark, the TSE 300. He was obviously fearful of being any more underweighted than that because of his own business risk.

We could solve his problem simply by changing his benchmark—to a unique version of the TSE 300, one where the weighting of any single stock in the index was truncated at X% of the total capitalization of the index. That unique index would implicitly be rebalanced each quarter, but that's a small price to pay to relieve the manager from a dysfunctional benchmark.

Some of the best *managers* are ones for whom there isn't a very good benchmark, and, in fact, they are not much concerned about benchmarks except in the very long run. These are *managers* who will invest our portfolio

---

[9]Joel Chernoff, *Pension & Investments*, August 7, 2000, p. 4.

however they think will make the most money. Their benchmark risk is gigantic. Categorizing such a *manager* in our asset allocation is fuzzy at best. Should we include such a *manager* on our team? By all means, *if* he is good enough. We should use benchmarks as tools, not as crutches.

How Much Excess Return to Expect

When our *adviser* waxes enthusiastic about a prospective *investment manager*, how much excess return[10] above his benchmark, net of fees, might we realistically expect long-term in the years ahead?

Over intervals of 10 to 20 years, net of fees, few *managers* of investment grade bonds can exceed the Lehman Aggregate Bond Index by as much as 1 percentage point per year, and few *managers* of large U.S. stocks can exceed the S&P 500 by 2 points per year. For less well-researched asset classes, I would be well pleased with 3 percentage points per year in excess of the relevant index. Considering the fact that we will inevitably choose some *managers* who are destined to underperform their benchmarks, I think we will be doing very well indeed if, in the aggregate over the long term, all of our active equity *managers* combined can succeed, net of fees, in beating their benchmarks by 1 to $1^1/_2$ percentage points per year.

Commingled Funds

Sometimes with a given manager we have a choice between a commingled fund or a separate account.[11] Which route should we take? Some investors like their own separate account whenever they can get it. My preference, however, would be for whichever approach is likely to achieve the best rate of return net of all costs, and that depends on the facts of the matter.

If we want something other than what the commingled fund is offering, the decision is easy: We can get it only with a separate account. But what if the manager invests the commingled fund and separate accounts in a similar manner?

---

[10]Sometimes, imprecisely, called "alpha."

[11]A commingled fund is one in which two or more clients invest. Group trusts and most limited partnerships are common examples. A mutual fund is an extreme example of a commingled fund. On the other hand, a separate account (except when the term is used by insurance companies) is an account held for only a single investor.

A commingled fund can often be preferable to a small separate account because the commingled fund is more diversified and is usually given more "showcase" management attention.

In short, neither a separate account nor a commingled fund is necessarily more advantageous than the other. It all depends.

How Many Managers?

To gain optimal diversification in common stocks, we have already discussed the importance of selecting outstanding *managers* in large stocks and small stocks, "growth" stocks and "value" stocks, and *managers* of U.S. stocks, stocks from the developed countries abroad, and stocks from the emerging markets. Also, we should have similar diversification among *managers* of the various fixed-income asset classes. Such diversification is the way to get the best long-term investment return with the lowest aggregate volatility.

A single manager would be most convenient for us—if it were the best in each of those specialties. But we have seldom seen managers who are considered the best in more than one or two of those specialties.

We should aim for outstanding *managers* in each of these areas. There is no magic number that's optimal. An extremely large fund can add further specialties to the above list—as long as the *managers* on its team are complementary to one another.

Upon finding two outstanding *managers* who ply the same turf, we may have a hard time deciding which to hire. Should we ease our problem by hiring both? If it's that close a call, flip a coin. Adding both might well add more complexity than value. Absolute return managers—such as market neutral and other hedge fund managers—are an exception, as a portfolio of such managers gives more consistent performance than any one of them.

There is, however, a reason other than diversification for having multiple *managers*. No matter how diligent the selection process, and how confident we are of our ultimate selection, every selection is a probability. If two-thirds of our selections turn out to be above-average performers, we'll be doing well. But let's not kid ourselves about our selections being error free. If we have only one or two *managers*, the impact of a *manager* who gives us disappointing performance is greater than if we have, say, 10 of them. With multiple *managers*, the probability of a home run declines, but (assuming a sound selection process) so do the odds of striking out.

What if we have only a $100,000 endowment fund? Or a *fund* with $20 million?

All too often, members of the investment committee know a local banker they trust, and they hire the bank's trust department to manage the endowment fund. The banker is usually highly trustworthy, indeed, but the approach is often submarginal—for two reasons:

1. Few bank trust departments have the expertise to invest with real global diversification, and

2. While the staff members of the bank trust departments work diligently at their jobs, they are rarely the best investors, for a very simple reason. Hardly any bank trust departments can afford the kind of compensation that will attract, or keep, the best.

Alternatively, many endowment funds place their money with a local investment management firm that has a strong reputation in the community. But the same questions should be raised: Does the firm have global expertise, and if so, is it really the best we can get in all areas? Few if any firms meet those criteria, anywhere.

Some brokers who sell mutual funds might tell us they provide consulting services for free, since the commissions cover their compensation. Their motivations can never be congruent with ours, however, since brokers are compensated on turnover—the amount of buying and selling in our portfolio—which by itself is irrelevant to us. Consultant remuneration based solely on a percentage of total assets managed would seem to align their motivations more closely with ours.

Well, how can a small endowment fund access the best managers? True, they can't be quite as sophisticated in their approach as large funds, but they can gain most of the benefits of diversification—thanks to mutual funds.

Among the thousands of mutual funds, there are world class funds in every category of marketable securities. Even an endowment fund as small as $50,000 or less can diversify among 10 highly diverse mutual funds.

Exclusive use of mutual funds would entail a marked change in policy for many *investment funds* that are either explicitly or implicitly wedded to the use of local investment management. There is no reason to discriminate against a local investment manager, but what should lead us to think that one or more of our local investment managers are among the best in the world? Our choice of *investment managers* should be blind as to where a manager's head office may be located. That blindness in itself is a key advantage of the exclusive use of mutual funds.

So much is published about mutual funds today in sources like *Morningstar* that we might try to select our mutual funds ourselves, without an *adviser*. Today, such an approach is more viable than ever, but I still would not advise it. An *adviser* should know a lot more about particular mutual funds than just what is published, and much of his value added is his subjective assessment of the predictive value of a mutual fund's track record.

In selecting mutual funds, we should have a sufficiently broad universe if we limit our choice to no-load mutual funds—funds that do not charge any brokerage commission for either buying or making withdrawals from the fund.[12]

Fees

When hiring a *manager*, we never know what his future performance will be. But we do know his fees. The *manager* must add value at least equal to his fees just to equal an index fund. So we must take fees seriously.

Let's recall a few facts of life. Great investment managers command high compensation—perhaps higher than warranted by their contribution to society in general. That's true also of star athletes, popular actors, and top corporate executives. Compensation is controlled by supply and demand, which means charging what the market will bear. If we place a low limit on our fee schedules for active management, we are likely to get no more than what we are paying for.

On the other hand, it doesn't work the other way. The only thing we know for sure is the fees we'll be paying. And paying high fees does not assure us of better long-term performance. In the end, what counts is only what we can spend—performance net of fees.

---

[12]In the selection of mutual funds, I also recommend sticking with funds that do *not* charge so-called "12(b)(1) fees." These fees equal up to 0.25%/year of assets and are used by a mutual fund for advertising and promotional purposes. The fees are permitted by the SEC in what I consider an inappropriate action by the SEC, because the fees clearly do not promote the interests of mutual fund investors. The fees enable a mutual fund to become larger, which in due course reduces the flexibility of its fund manager to perform. There is an ample supply of good mutual funds with the integrity not to charge 12(b)(1) fees, and I would stick with them.

RETAINING MANAGERS

"Managing investment managers is easy," asserted a chief financial officer I met back in the 1970s. "Each year we simply fire the managers with the worst two records over the last three years."

Oh, if only it were that simple!

At least once each year, our *adviser* should review each individual *manager* with the investment committee The review should cover not only performance but also why the *manager* still fits our criteria for hiring and retaining *managers*. In particular, the *adviser* should explain why he still considers the *manager* the best we can get in its asset class.

When to Take Action

Adding or withdrawing assets to or from a *manager's* account should not be a sign that we have made a positive or negative evaluation of a *manager*. We may increase an account's assets as the result of a new contribution to the plan, or a transfer of assets from another account that had become over-weighted relative to its target. We may periodically have to withdraw assets from an account to raise money to make payments to our sponsor or to pensioners. More often, such actions simply reflect efforts to adjust the allocation of total plan assets closer to the Policy Asset Allocation.

I do not advocate withdrawing a portion of a manager's account simply because we have given him a poor evaluation. Investment managers do not need a wake-up call. Any manager worth his salt is going all-out continuously and knows when he is not performing well. He cannot perform better simply by working harder. If he's performing poorly, he is probably hurting even more than we are. We can't possibly flagellate him into better performance. If we have lost confidence in a *manager*, we should terminate his account.

On one or two occasions, I have heard sponsors consider giving a manager a warning, something like, "We'll give you X quarters to straighten out your performance, or we'll have to terminate the account." While it's essential to be honest with our managers, I believe such a warning is never appropriate. First of all, we can never know whether his (short-term) performance during the warning period has any predictive value. And second, the manager gets an absolutely wrong motivation: "We must do something, anything, because if we do nothing we will lose the account. And if we do something, maybe we'll get lucky." We never want to motivate our manager to roll the dice.

When to Terminate a *Manager's* Account

Reasons for termination may fit under five overlapping headings:

1. We lose trust in the *manager*. If we believe a manager is being less than honest with us, or if he fails to honor agreements with us, it is time to part company. Trust is a sine qua non of our relationship with any *manager*.

2. We lose confidence that a *manager* can add much value to his benchmark. What would cause us to lose confidence?
   - Performance is below benchmark
     - for a meaningful interval
     - by a sufficient magnitude, and
     - for reasons not explainable by investment style such as market cap, or growth vs. value

     so we can no longer objectively expect that the *manager* is likely to exceed his benchmark materially in the future.
   - The *manager's* performance has become inexplicably erratic.

3. Even though a *manager's* performance remains satisfactory, its predictive value declines materially. This judgment is rarely based on a single factor. It is influenced by factors such as the following:
   - A key person (or persons) left our account.
   - The *manager* embarked on a different management approach than that on which his track record is based.
   - The *manager* is now managing much more money than that on which his track record is based, and we believe this added money will impair his future performance.

4. We find another *manager* we believe would add materially more value than an existing *manager* in the same niche, even though the existing *manager* has done well for us.

5. Here are two reasons related to our diversification needs:
   - We perceive that two of our *managers* in the same asset class are pursuing the same investment style.
   - We have reduced our Policy Allocation to a particular asset class to an extent where we no longer find it important to have as many *managers* in that asset class.

Much of this comes down to assessing the *manager's* likely performance in the years ahead. Assessing that requires tough objectivity of all relevant facts. The key word is *relevant*. Figuring out what's relevant and what's not for a particular *manager* is a major challenge, and if we get it wrong, we are likely to take the wrong action.

Rebalancing

Once we have gotten the actual asset allocation of our portfolio to be the same as our Policy Asset Allocation, it won't stay that way. One asset class will perform better than another, and we'll soon be off target. We should rebalance periodically to our Policy Allocation. This periodic rebalancing forces us to do something that is not intuitively comfortable—sell from asset classes that have performed best and reinvest the proceeds in those that have performed worst.

David Swensen has articulated clearly the case for rebalancing: "Far too many investors spend enormous amounts of time and energy constructing policy portfolios, only to allow the allocations they established to drift with the whims of the market. . . . Without a disciplined approach to maintain policy targets, fiduciaries fail to achieve the desired characteristics for the institution's portfolio."[13]

Many plan sponsors set ranges for their Policy Asset Allocations—such as 20% plus or minus 5%. The market could drive such an asset class mighty far from its 20% target before the plan sponsor would be motivated to take some action.

My preference is for a pinpoint target for each asset class—X% of the portfolio. No range. And when the market drives the asset class away from that target, let's rebalance to bring it back. Why?

- If the outperformance of a particular asset class gave any valid prediction that the same asset class would outperform in the next interval of time, that would be a valid reason for utilizing a range. But that is not the case. Outperformance by Asset Class A in Interval 1 gives almost zero information about its performance in Interval 2— with one exception. One of the pervasive dynamics in investments is reversion to the mean, and sooner or later Asset Class A will begin to underperform.

---

[13]Swensen, *Pioneering*, p. 4.

Hence, over the long term, rebalancing to a target may add a tiny increment of return by forcing us, on average, to buy low and sell high. That can be a counterintuitive discipline, of course—adding money to an asset class (and therefore to *managers*) who have been less successful lately, and taking it away from stellar performers. But it makes sense, provided we retain high confidence in all our *managers*.

- If we were confident we could predict with reasonable accuracy which asset class would outperform or underperform others in Interval 2, then we should take advantage of tactical asset allocation insights. I, for one, have no such confidence, and I don't tend to have much confidence in such insights of others. Unless we justifiably have that confidence, rebalancing is the way to go.

  We can spend a lot of time agonizing over where to take that withdrawal we need, or where to place our latest contribution. A rebalancing discipline removes a good deal of the agonizing and also makes good sense.

- Presumably we established our Policy Asset Allocation in order to earn the best expected return for a given level of aggregate portfolio risk. To the extent we stray from our Policy Allocation, we are probably straying from our target portfolio risk and from the Efficient Frontier.

Doesn't rebalancing incur unnecessary transaction costs? It doesn't have to. If we have sizable amounts of contributions to or withdrawals from our fund, we can probably rebalance without any incremental costs—simply by using those cash flows to rebalance. Or if we invest in no-load mutual funds or commingled funds, we can usually rebalance without cost to us. Or if we use index funds, we can keep part of our assets in index futures, which we can rebalance at little cost.

But what if rebalancing will necessitate additional transactions by some of our investment managers?

We can actually execute such transactions with minimal incremental cost if we give our manager enough notice. If we tell a manager, "we will need $10 million from our $100 million account any time in the next three months," he can often raise much of that $10 million through his normal transactions during that quarter, simply by his not reinvesting proceeds from his routine sales.

Even if we can rebalance entirely from the withdrawals we must take from our fund periodically to pay pension benefits or endowment income, we should still forecast our cash needs well in advance and try to give our managers a few months, if possible, to raise the cash. All for the purpose of minimizing transaction costs.

How often should we rebalance?

There have been some good academic studies on rebalancing. Some suggest we might be ahead by adopting a quarterly discipline. Others seem to suggest that there is little difference between doing it once a quarter or once a year. Still others suggest not more than once a year. Yet others indicate that use of a target range is best. Differences in results of the studies depend on the particular time intervals of the studies. I favor doing it continuously with cash flow and then taking action once a year if we are still materially off our Policy Allocation.

How about rebalancing managers within the same asset class? If two managers are in two different subclasses, such as large-cap growth and large-cap value, I think rebalancing makes sense. If two managers are in the very same asset class, well, I haven't seen scholarly studies on that, and I think that's up to our qualitative judgment on a case-by-case basis, but rebalancing between them may make the best sense.

The most important point is to have a rebalancing plan and stick to it, with exceptions rarely more frequent than once in 10 years.

IN SHORT

- Once we have established our portfolio's Policy Asset Allocation, we then want the best *managers* we can get in each individual asset class. This typically means a relatively large number of *managers*.
- As committee members, we should know the criteria for hiring and retaining each *manager* and be prepared to question our *adviser* on the basis of these criteria.
- We should know at least as much about our existing *managers* as about *managers* we are considering to hire, and we should ask each year if our existing *managers* are still the best we can get.

CHAPTER **7**

The Custodian

No matter how small, an *investment fund* with multiple managers should have a custodian. Why?

A custodian safeguards the assets. It sees that every penny is always invested, at least in a money market fund if not otherwise directed. It executes all transactions as directed and provides regular transaction reports and asset statements.

Yes, it is possible for a tiny *investment fund* to own shares in multiple mutual fund accounts without a custodian, but it places a burden on the sponsor's small staff or a volunteer board member. And even if they can do the job well, their successors may not be as competent in that task.

If the *investment fund* has one or more separately managed accounts (as opposed to mutual funds), a custodian is a must. For one thing, it separates the function of custody from that of investment management. The investment manager doesn't get its hands on any assets. Nobody at the manager's firm can abscond with any assets as long as custody is with a different party. Nor can it lie to us about the assets it is managing for us. For most kinds of skullduggery, the trustee and investment manager (or their staff people) would have to collude—a less likely occurrence. Some notorious cases of fraud could hardly have happened if the client had used a custodian.

The custodian is usually a bank, although the task might feasibly be done by a broker or even a consultant. One advantage of the bank is that the assets never belong to the bank. If the bank ever went bankrupt, its creditors could not get their hands on any of our assets. This is not true of a broker who holds client assets in a custody account, because the assets in that custody account are in the broker's name. If the broker ever went bankrupt, our assets would be in jeopardy.

A tiny *investment fund* will want to find the lowest-cost custodian, perhaps from its local bank. The fund will receive transaction reports and asset statements, but probably little else. Without paying extra, it will not receive performance reports or other analyses, and it may not need them if it has a consultant who can provide those services.

CUSTODIAL REPORTING

At the end of each month, a sophisticated custodian provides the client the following statements for each account and for the overall *fund*:

- An asset statement showing the month-end book value and market value, usually categorized into convenient asset groupings selected by the client, with subtotals for each grouping.
- A list of all transactions, including those that were accrued but not settled at the end of the month. Accrued transactions are noted on the asset statement as "Accounts Payable" and "Accounts Receivable."
- For each account, a daily log of all purchases and sales of securities during the month, as well as all contributions and all withdrawals or expenses paid at the direction of the fund's sponsor.
- A list of all income (interest and dividend payments) received.
- A list of all cash flows into (contributions) and out of (disbursements) the *fund*.
- Foreign investments are shown in terms of both local and U.S. currency.
- Special reports requested by the client, such as aggregate brokerage commission reports, or a listing of the largest 10 transactions during the month.

For an *investment fund* with separately managed accounts, we might require that the custodian send a copy of each account's monthly statement to the manager of that account, and that the manager, within two weeks of receipt, review that statement and write a letter to the custodian (with a copy to our *adviser*) saying either (1) the manager agrees entirely with the custodian's statement, or (2) it agrees except for the following items (and then lists each variance). The custodian and manager must then get together and resolve each variance, again with a copy to the *adviser* explaining the resolution. This procedure serves to improve the accuracy of both the custodian's and manager's records. The *adviser's* task is that of monitoring the mail—to make sure each manager responds to the custodian each month, and that each item of variance is resolved.

Why do I like this process? No one knows more than the manager about his particular assets and transactions. He is aware of more nuances than any outside auditor. Also, he has a vested interest in keeping the custodian's records accurate, because he knows we are relying on the custodian's statements, not his (the manager's). Moreover, any errors in the custodian's records can affect the calculation of investment performance, perhaps the most important management information of all.

The custodian will provide another important service: For an organization with multiple restricted endowments or multiple pension plans that the organization commingles for purposes of investment, a custodian can provide the unitized recordkeeping—like the recordkeeping for a mutual fund.

The custodian also prepares and files tax returns and special government reports as necessary.

Custodianship today is a highly capital-intensive industry—with the capital all going into systems and software to carry out the trustee's monumental information-processing function. The needed capital can run into hundreds of millions of dollars. Much of this capital investment is for the provision of management information, which we will discuss next.

MANAGEMENT INFORMATION

Given all the raw data that a custodian has about every investment account, no one is better situated to provide us with analyses of performance and the composition of individual investment accounts and our overall investment account. Besides the usual performance charts that are regularly presented at committee meetings, the sophisticated custodian can provide our *adviser* with a range of analytics that is as broad as one's imagination.

The more sophisticated master custodians, with all of the raw data in their computers, have over the years developed reliable and flexible performance measurement systems. A good trustee keeps track of some 2,000 different indexes and combinations of indexes for use as benchmarks, as requested by its various clients. And it can compare our *fund's* performance against a universe of other endowment or pension funds. The custodian can then present this information in any number of graphic forms.

The more sophisticated custodian can slice and dice the composition of any particular portfolio by virtually any measure one can imagine—by industry, by country, by price/earnings ratio, by market capitalization, and by innumerable other measures. And it can display these in a wide range of graphic forms.

The convenience afforded by having all of our plan's assets under one roof gives us, the plan sponsor, remarkable flexibility. We can do things easily that would be difficult or impossible to do without a custodian. For example:

- If we terminate a manager, we simply have to instruct our custodian not to accept any more transactions from the terminated manager, and then place the assets in the account under the direction of a new manager.
- If we have a manager of foreign exchange (FX) who is authorized to hedge all foreign currency exposure that is not otherwise hedged, our trustee can provide our FX manager a daily list of the total unhedged dollar exposure of our composite account to each foreign currency.
- We can have all of our assets made available to a single securities-lending agent—the most convenient agent often being the master custodian itself.

Each of these management information services comes, of course, with a price tag. Our *adviser* can help us select a custodian and also which management information services would seem worth subscribing to.

IN SHORT

- Every *investment fund* should have a custodian, usually a bank.
- The custodian safeguards the assets and provides transaction reports and asset listings showing book values and market values.
- The custodian can also be a valuable source of management information, such as performance measurement and portfolio composition.

CHAPTER 8

Evaluating an
Investment Fund's Organization

If I were asked to evaluate the organization of an *investment fund*, how would I go about it?

I'd be interested in prior performance, of course, but that is only prologue. Past performance, either absolute or relative to peers, is not by itself a valid criterion. Good past performance might be the fortuitous result of a poorly designed investment program, and poor past performance might be the random result of a well-designed investment program.

The only thing that counts is the future. Hence, our evaluation should be future oriented. We will want all the quantitative measures that are relevant. But ultimately, an evaluation comes down to asking the right questions and concluding with qualitative judgments. What are some of the right questions? My suggestions follow.

INVESTMENT OBJECTIVES

- Does the *fund* have a written statement of Investment Policies? Are they well thought out?
- Do all key decision makers buy into these policies, and do they understand their ramifications?
- Do the Investment Policies define an overall risk constraint? Why and how was the measure of risk chosen?
- Is the risk constraint appropriate for the *fund* sponsor's financial situation?
- Is the investment return objective defined as the highest return that can be achieved within that risk constraint?

- How long have these objectives been in effect?
- Net of all costs, how well have these objectives been met?

ASSET ALLOCATION

- What is the Policy Asset Allocation?
- What was the rationale underlying this asset allocation?
- How close is the Policy Asset Allocation to an Efficient Frontier?
- Were adequate sensitivity tests on risk, return, and correlation assumptions carried out in Efficient Frontier studies?
- How many diverse asset classes were included in the Efficient Frontier study?
- How many asset classes is the *adviser* prepared competently to recommend and manage?
- How close has the *fund's* actual allocation been to its Policy Allocation?
- Does the plan diverge from its Policy Asset Allocation tactically? If so, who decides? With what results?
- How does the *fund* go about rebalancing?

THE FIDUCIARY COMMITTEE

- Does the *fund* have a written statement of Operating Policies?
- Who are the members of the *fund's* fiduciary committee? What are the criteria for membership, and why?
- How much experience do the members have in institutional portfolio investing, and how much time each year do they devote to this function?
- Is the fiduciary committee sufficiently oriented to the long-term, or is it overly concerned with short-term performance?
- What decisions does the committee reserve for itself, and what decisions does it delegate to its *adviser*? Why?
- How much confidence does the committee have in its *adviser*?

- What constraints does the committee place on its *adviser*—either through limits on its openness to new ideas or the frequency of its meetings?
- How does the committee judge the effectiveness of its *adviser*?

THE *ADVISER*

- How experienced is the *adviser*? What is its size, its continuity, and its commitment to excellence?
- How does it go about retaining good people?
- How able is it to advise on asset allocation? What are its processes for this?
- How able is it to evaluate alternative investments such as those described in Chapter 5?
- How well-researched and supported are its recommendations (or actions)?
- How well does it communicate with the investment committee?
- How well does it do in the continuous education of committee members?
- How does the *adviser* monitor each of the *fund's managers* and maintain an up-to-date understanding of all the factors that impact the predictive value of that *manager's* past performance?
- What triggers a recommendation to terminate a *manager*?
- What is the rationale for retaining each of the *fund's* current *managers*?
- How does the *adviser* go about finding out whether there are better *managers* available that it might be using?
- How solid are the *adviser's* administrative support services?
- What steps has it taken to mitigate manager risks? What are its audit procedures? How does it control managers' use of derivatives? How much possibility is there for a manager to penetrate the *fund's* deep pockets?
- In each asset class, was an index fund considered? Why or why not was an index fund chosen?
- What do the *adviser's* other clients say about their experience with the *adviser*? What has been the *adviser's* client turnover?

INVESTMENT MANAGERS

- In each asset class, net of all costs, how have the fund's active *managers*—including terminated *managers*—performed relative to an index fund alternative? How have they performed relative to other active *managers*?
- Has the *fund* stayed within its overall risk constraint?
- If the fund's historic risk has been materially below its overall risk constraint, could performance have been improved by taking more risk, closer to the fund's overall risk constraint?

CHAPTER 9

Structure of an Endowment Fund

What is the purpose of an endowment fund or foundation? Its purpose is to throw off a perpetual stream of income to support the operations of the sponsoring organization. All endowment policies should flow from that purpose.

Key criteria for endowments:

- For planning and budgeting purposes, the stream of income should be reasonably predictable.
- For the health of the organization, the magnitude of that stream of income should, over the long term, maintain its buying power. "While fiduciary principles generally specify only that the institution preserve the nominal value of a gift, to provide true permanent support, institutions must maintain the inflation-adjusted value of a gift," writes David Swensen of the Yale endowment fund.[1]

THE TOTAL RETURN, OR IMPUTED INCOME, APPROACH

If your organization is already using the Imputed Income approach to determine the amount of money to transfer each year from the your endowment fund to your sponsor's operating account, you may care to skip this section.

The traditional approach to income recognition by endowment funds is

---

[1]David F. Swensen, *Pioneering Portfolio Managment* (The Free Press, 2000), p. 27.

materially flawed. It defines income by the accounting definition of dividends, interest, rent, and sometimes net realized capital gains as well. If an investment approach is kept reasonably intact, the year-to-year stream of dividends, interest, and rent is quite predictable. But the impact on income is a key consideration if anyone suggests a major change in the endowment's investment approach. Moreover, if realized capital gains are included in the definition of income, that creates a wild card.

The trouble with income defined as just dividends, interest, and rent is that it impacts investment policy both seriously and detrimentally. To provide a reasonable amount of income, the sponsor is motivated to invest a major proportion of the endowment in bonds and stocks that pay high interest or dividends. And if income is running short of what is needed, the sponsor can adjust the investment portfolio to increase the dividends and interest.

Such an approach dooms the second criterion, of maintaining the endowment's buying power over the long term. That's because the market value of bonds, for example, does nothing to maintain buying power (unless one considers relatively new inflation-linked bonds). There is no concept of real return—investment return in excess of inflation.

Because the definition of income has such a great impact on investment policies, the definition of income must be revised before we can consider investment policy.

Fortunately, a concept has been developed that does a pretty good job of meeting both of the above criteria, and it is widely used today. It is known as the "Total Return" or "Imputed Income" approach.

The Total Return Approach begins with the concept that we should recognize as income only an amount that might, long-term, be considered real income—income in excess of inflation. So the first question is: How much real return can we realistically aspire to earn on our endowment fund over the long term?

That depends on how we invest the endowment fund. It's obvious, then, that the way to maximize the endowment's real return over the long term is to maximize its total return—the sum of accounting income plus capital gains, both realized and unrealized. We go right back to Chapters 3 and 4, "Investment Objectives" and "Asset Allocation," as they are the starting point.

Let's say we decide on an asset mix of 80% common stocks, 20% fixed income, or 75/25, and after consulting historical returns of those asset classes, we conclude that we can prudently expect a real return over the long term of 5% per year. That says we can recognize 5% of market value as "Imputed Income" each year.

But with this asset allocation the market value will fluctuate widely from year to year, and if Imputed Income equals 5% of that fluctuating value, then the fluctuations in annual income may be greater than our sponsor can live with. Therefore, let's define Imputed Income as 5% of a moving average of market values. While there are many variations, we have found that a sound definition of Imputed Income is: X% of the average market value of the endowment fund over the last five year-ends (adjusted for new contributions and adjusted for withdrawals in excess of Imputed Income, if any).

Appendix 9 at the end of this chapter describes how the Imputed Income method works. This approach includes the following advantages:

- The sponsor gains a fairly predictable level of annual income, not subject to large percentage changes from year to year.
- The sponsor learns early in the year the amount of income it will withdraw from the endowment fund. This is a big help in budgeting.
- Investment policy cannot be manipulated. The only way our sponsor can increase Imputed Income is by investing more successfully—by achieving a higher rate of total return, long term.

What is the downside of the Total Return Approach? There may be intervals when the fund's market value declines for several years in a row, and the dollar amount of Imputed Income may actually decline. There is no way to avoid this possibility, since all markets are volatile. But markets, over a great many years, have eventually bounced back each time. As they do, the fund, under the Total Return Approach, should regain the buying power that it lost—provided the rate of Imputed Income was established responsibly in the first place.

Once the sponsor knows the amount of Imputed Income for the current year, it can decide when during the year it will withdraw the money. A withdrawal usually requires a sale of stocks or bonds (or mutual funds), since cash should not generally be allowed to accumulate. Dividends and interest should be reinvested promptly.

Warning: Members of the fund sponsor may agitate to raise the Imputed Income percentage, and clamor hardest at the wrong time. For example, during the 20-year intervals ending in the late 1990s, investment returns far exceeded the 5% real return assumption that formed the philosophical basis for the Imputed Income formula of many endowment funds. At that time, members of certain fund sponsors agitated successfully to raise the Imputed Income percentage to $5^1/_2\%$ or 6%— just before the market plunged in 2000–2002. It is easy to forget that a market debacle like that has occurred before and will occur sometime again. The higher the market goes, the higher the probability that it will occur. My advice, therefore is: Don't make a change. If we have established our Imputed Income formula soundly in the first place, let's not tinker with it.

David Swensen of the Yale endowment fund has articulated the danger well: "Increases in spending soon become part of an institution's permanent expense base, reducing operational flexibility. If the rate of spending rises in a boom, an institution facing a bust loses the benefit of a cushion and gains the burden of a greater budgetary base."[2]

"OWNERS" OF THE ENDOWMENT FUND

We speak of a sponsor's endowment fund as if that sponsor were the sole owner. That's true in one sense, but it's a little more complicated than that. There are two basic kinds of money in the endowment fund.

- Donor Designated
- Board Designated

Donor Designated endowment is money that was designated by the contributor for the purpose of endowment. Legally, that is the only true endowment. To keep faith with its contributors, and the law, the sponsor should withdraw no more than annual income; the sponsor may not withdraw principal. Under most endowment statutes, Imputed Income meets this requirement of not withdrawing more than annual income, provided the definition of Imputed Income has been established rationally. In fact, I would contend that the Imputed Income approach meets the intent of endowment statutes far better than the traditional definition of income (interest and dividends, etc.).

---

[2]Ibid., p. 38.

Board Designated money is money the sponsor's board of directors chose to treat as endowment. It is not legally endowment, and future boards may at any time withdraw the entire principal if they so choose, since one board cannot bind a future board in this regard. But the sponsor has every reason to treat Board Designated endowment as true endowment, investing it with a long-term approach in the hope and assumption that future boards will treat it similarly.

Why would a sponsor's board choose to designate new contributions as endowment?

- Many sponsors encourage their supporters to include the sponsor in their wills. Bequests are a wonderful support for any sponsor. But bequests come in lumpy fashion—a whole lot one year, very little the next, with no way of predicting the pattern. Few bequests are designated by the donor specifically for endowment. But bequests should generally not be put into the operating budget, since they can't be budgeted for. Hence many sponsors have a standing board resolution that all bequests are automatically to go into endowment.
- Sponsors receive other unexpected gifts during the year, such as gifts in memory of a supporter who has just died. These also are best shunted directly to endowment.
- If the sponsor is fortunate to end a year with a budget surplus, one of the things the sponsor might consider doing with the surplus is directing it to endowment, where it can benefit the sponsor for years to come rather than artificially easing the sponsor's operating budget for just the coming year.

Use-Restricted Endowment

Many donors restrict their contributions to particular uses that are important to them. For example, a sponsor might receive two large contributions—one simply restricted to Program X, and the other designated for endowment *and also* restricted to Program X.

The sponsor would now have four endowment fund "owners":

1. *Donor Designated, Restricted to Program X*: The donor designated the gift to endowment and restricted it to Program X.

2. *Donor Designated, Unrestricted*: The donor designated the gift to endowment but didn't restrict its use to any particular program.

3. *Board Designated, Restricted to Program X*: The donor restricted the gift to Program X but the board, not the donor, designated it to endowment.

4. *Board Designated, Unrestricted*: The donor didn't restrict the gift to any program, and the board, not the donor, designated it to endowment.

A large sponsor, such as a university, could conceivably have dozens of restricted endowments, some of them Donor Designated, and some Board Designated. Each of these endowments must be accounted for separately, so that the income from each can be used for its particular purpose.

If we have a dozen such endowments, we can invest each separately, receiving from our custodian a separate statement on each. Or we can do things a simpler way, a way that both saves cost and leads to better investment returns: We can coinvest all such endowments as a single endowment fund.

But then how do we keep each endowment separate? Through unit accounting, just like a mutual fund. That means we must unitize our endowment fund. Each of the "owners" of the endowment fund is credited with units every time a contribution is made for that owner, just as we are credited with shares every time we buy a mutual fund, and vice versa for withdrawals. That way, the value of the endowment fund held for each "owner" is kept distinct regardless of how diverse the contributions and withdrawals on behalf of each "owner".

IN SHORT

- An endowment fund is intended to provide perpetual annual income to its sponsor. That annual income should be reasonably predictable and over the long term should at least maintain its buying power.

- Our endowment fund can best meet these objectives if annual income is calculated under the Total Return, or Imputed Income, approach— such as a reasonable percentage of the fund's average market value over the last five years.

APPENDIX 9
The Total Return or Imputed Income Method

1. For any fiscal year, Imputed Income equal to 5% of the Base Market Value of the Endowment Fund shall be withdrawn and realized as income for that year.

2. The Base Market Value shall be the average market value of the Endowment Fund on December 31 of the last five calendar years. The market value at prior year-ends, however, shall be increased for contributions (or decreased for withdrawals, if any, other than withdrawals of Imputed Income) made subsequent to those years according to the following procedure: A contribution (or special withdrawal other than Imputed Income) shall be valued at 95% for the first year-end prior to the contribution (or special withdrawal); 90% for the second prior year-end; 85% for the third prior year-end; and 80% for the fourth prior year-end.[3]

3. The timing of withdrawals of Imputed Income during each fiscal year shall be at the discretion of the Finance Committee. At the time an Imputed Income withdrawal is to be made, the Investment Committee shall decide from which *investment manager(s)* the withdrawal shall be made. If a separately managed account does not hold enough cash to meet the withdrawal, the manager of that account shall sell assets sufficient to meet the withdrawal.

4. Withdrawals of Imputed Income shall be allocated to the accounts of the various owners of the endowment fund[4] on the basis of the relative market values of those owners' accounts as of the latest year-end.

   On the following page is a sample Imputed Income worksheet.

---

[3]If we don't adjust prior yearend market values for subsequent contributions, the effect would be to take only 1% (1/5 × 5%) of a new contribution in year one, because the latest year-end market value determines only one-fifth of Base Market Value. Similarly the effect would be 2% in year two, 3% in year three, etc.

[4]Such as "Donor Designated, Restricted to Program X," or "Board Designated, Unrestricted."

Sample Imputed Income Worksheet

Columns 12/31/96 – 12/31/05 fall under the spanning heading **Adjusted Year-End Market Values**.

Date	Entry	Market Value	Net Contributions	12/31/96	12/31/97	12/31/98	12/31/99	12/31/00	12/31/01	12/31/02	12/31/03	12/31/04	12/31/05	5-Yr. Total	Imputed Income
12/31/99	MV	0		80,000	85,000	90,000	95,000	100,000							
Year '00	C		100,000	80,000	85,000	90,000	95,000	100,000						450,000	4,500
12/31/00	MV	100,000			45,200	48,025	50,850	53,675	56,500						
Year '01	C		56,500		130,200	138,025	145,850	153,675	165,816					733,566	7,336
12/31/01	MV	165,816				440,000	467,500	495,000	522,500	550,000					
Year '02	C		550,000			578,025	613,350	648,675	688,316	800,000				3,328,366	33,284
12/31/02	MV	800,000					240,000	255,000	270,000	285,000	300,000				
Year '03	C		300,000				853,350	903,675	958,316	1,085,000	1,210,000			5,010,341	50,103
12/31/03	MV	1,210,000						6,400	6,800	7,200	7,600	8,000			
Year '04	C		8,000					910,075	965,116	1,092,200	1,217,600	1,210,000		5,394,991	53,950
12/31/04	MV	1,210,000							9,600	10,200	10,800	11,400	12,000		
Year '05	C		12,000						974,716	1,102,400	1,228,400	1,221,400	1,390,000	5,916,916	59,169
12/31/05	MV	1,390,000													

C = Net Contributions (net of any withdrawals other than of Imputed Income)

MV = Market Value

Last column = 1/5 of 5-Yr. Total, times 5%

CHAPTER 10

What's Different about Pension Funds?

Preface: "Pension plan," as used in this chapter, will refer only to defined-benefit pension plans, not defined-contribution pension plans.

A defined-benefit plan is a traditional pension plan, where the benefit is defined as an annuity—$X a month for the rest of our life—or a cash balance pension plan, where the benefit is defined as a lump sum. In either case, the plan sponsor bears the entire risk or opportunity of investment results. The employee is entirely unaffected.

A defined contribution plan, such as a 401(k) plan, is one where the employee bears the entire risk or opportunity of investment results. Within the investment options provided by the plan, the employee decides how his particular account will be invested.

First, what's similar about pension funds and endowments? Most things. They both want the highest long-term return they can achieve within an acceptable level of risk. The process of developing their investment policy and asset allocation, and hiring and monitoring *managers*, is essentially the same, and so are the principles of governance. In fact, almost everything written in the first eight chapters of this book applies to pension funds as well as endowment funds.

So what's different (besides the fact that private pension plans are governed by ERISA)? A pension plan's definition of risk should be different. For the endowment fund, risk is the volatility in the market value of its portfolio. For pension funds, risk is the possibility that the plan won't be able to pay all promised pension benefits to retirees. As long as the plan sponsor remains solvent, that's not much of a risk, because if pension assets fall short of pension liabilities, the plan sponsor must make higher contributions to the pension fund. So risk for the plan sponsor is just that—the possibility of the sponsor having to make greater contributions to the pension fund, perhaps suddenly much higher.[1]

A measure of risk for the pension plan therefore is its *funding ratio*— the ratio of the market value of plan assets to the present value of the plan's liabilities, and *both* change from year to year. That's because a declining funding ratio means the plan sponsor will have to come up with higher contributions to the plan.

PENSION PLAN LIABILITIES

In truth, the promises the pension plan has made to its participants don't really change much from year to year. They change only by the amount of additional benefits employees have accrued each year. What changes is the *present value* of those promises. What do we mean by present value?

If we promise to pay someone $1,000 ten years from now, what is our liability today? Certainly not $1,000. We could put a lesser amount in the bank today, and that would grow into the $1,000 we need 10 years from now. That lesser amount, realistically, is our liability today. The amount we need today—the present value—depends on what rate of interest we expect we can earn. And reasonable people can't agree on what rate of interest we should assume.

Financial accounting standards say the interest rate assumption should vary each year depending on the change in the prevailing interest rate on corporate bonds. That's the interest assumption that determines the present value of pension liabilities shown in a company's annual report. The Pension Benefit Guarantee Corporation, as an insurance company, uses an interest rate more closely related to the interest rate on long government

---

[1]If pension assets fall short and the sponsor becomes insolvent, then the risk falls upon the insurer—the federally chartered Pension Benefit Guarantee Corporation.

bonds. That results in a much higher present value of pension liabilities. For other purposes, other interest assumptions are made.

The key point is that pension liabilities change each year with interest rates. As interest rates go down, liabilities go up. And vice versa. So trying to maintain a level funding ratio—the ratio of assets to liabilities—is a moving target. The market value of assets may have risen nicely last year, but our plan's funding ratio might be down if interest rates have dropped sharply at the same time.

INVESTMENT IMPLICATIONS

What does this mean for the investment of a pension portfolio? It means that risk is not just the volatility in the market values of assets but also in the volatility in interest rates. A nice safe T-bill may be anything but safe for a pension plan, because its future value is quite unpredictable relative to the present value of pension liabilities.

What's the safest asset for a pension plan relative to the plan's liabilities? It's a very long-term government bond, whose market value is extremely volatile. But the volatility of its market value moves in synch with the volatility in plan liabilities.

Given this complication, how do we develop the Policy Asset Allocation for our pension plan? The best way is to do an asset/liability study. This study requires the same set of assumptions we discussed in Chapter 4 for an Efficient Frontier. The study also includes a projection of plan liabilities. It uses 500 or more Monte Carlo simulations to project the range of probabilities for funding ratios, future contributions, and the present value of all future contributions. Based on these definitions of risk, the study also indicates an Efficient Frontier for each set of assumptions, and it also provides useful probabilities of unhappy results from any given asset allocation.

Asset/liability studies are much more complex and expensive than simple Efficient Frontier studies, and modest-size pension plans may feel they can't afford one. What are the main differences in the output?

The asset/liability study will recommend that all traditional fixed income be allocated to very long durations, but in other ways its recommended asset allocations are often not greatly different from those indicated by a simple Efficient Frontier study. The amount and duration of the allocation to long-term fixed income will depend on the nature of liabilities. If the pension plan is for a younger work force, the duration of liabilities will be very long, and so might be the allocation to bonds. If the plan is largely for older or retired employees, duration will not be quite as long.

IN SHORT

- The sole purpose of a pension fund is to pay promised pension benefits. Those promised benefits are its liabilities.
- We can best decide the Policy Asset Allocation of our pension fund with the help of an asset/liability study.
- Such a study will typically show that the least risky asset class for our pension fund is not cash, but high-quality bonds of very long duration.

CHAPTER 11

Once Again

Members of an investment committee need not be experts, but they should have some familiarity with investments. They should have open minds and be willing to learn. They should make a commitment to attend all meetings they possibly can and to review carefully any materials distributed in preparation for those meetings. The committee chairman should be a strong leader who is focused, able to keep discussion on track, and can bring committee members to final resolution on issues.

We committee members devote a relatively few hours per year to the *fund's* investments and should not try to go it alone. We need an *adviser*. We should hire a chief investment officer and staff, if the *fund* is large enough to afford it, or else hire a consultant on whom we can rely for education, recommendations, and reporting performance. If the *fund* is too small to afford a consultant, we should recruit a committee member with experience in portfolio management who will serve the function of a consultant.

We should first establish a written Operating Policy, covering the committee's procedures and responsibilities. We should also appoint a custodian (usually a trust company) that will hold all of the *fund's* assets and provide timely reports on the *fund's* market values.

Our most important task is to establish a written Investment Policy. This statement should include a Policy Asset Allocation and benchmarks for each asset class included in that Policy Asset Allocation. Our asset allocation will have far more impact on the *fund's* future investment returns than any other action we will take, including the selection of *investment managers*. The range of asset classes we should include in that Policy Asset Allocation far exceeds traditional ones of domestic stocks, bonds, and cash.

To the extent that we make use of all attractive asset classes we can, the additional diversification can meaningfully reduce the *fund's* volatility and even ratchet up its expected return.

It is okay to be aware of conventional investment wisdom—what our peer endowment or pension funds are doing. But let's not become prisoners of their investment objectives and constraints, or use them as our principal benchmarks. Let's do our own independent thinking as we set our Investment Policies and select our *investment managers*.

Only after deciding on our Policy Asset Allocation should we consider who will be our *investment managers*. Our objective should be to hire the best possible manager(s) for each asset class. Rarely does an investment firm qualify as the best possible *manager* in more than one asset class, so we should be prepared to hire multiple managers (or invest in multiple investment funds), often more than a dozen, even for a very small *fund*.

Before selecting a *manager*, we should first decide whether to use an index fund or active management for that asset class.

Our *adviser* should recommend individual *managers*, but we committee members should learn the criteria for hiring and retaining *managers* and be prepared to question our *adviser* on the basis of those criteria.

We should know at least as much about our existing *managers* as about a *manager* we are considering to hire, and every year we should ask our *adviser* if each of our existing *managers* is still the best we can get for that particular asset class.

If we have a broadly diversified portfolio, as we should, we will have some risky investments. If one of those risky investments should turn sour, what protection do we have against charges of imprudence? We should do two things:

1. I can't overemphasize: Avoid even the perception of conflict of interest.
2. Maintain good records about:
    a. Why each investment decision was made, including a copy of the full presentation made to the committee, and

   b. The periodic review of our *investment managers* and why the retention of each *manager* was appropriate.

Prudence is not a matter of what happened to an investment with 20/20 hindsight. It's the process and rationale that went into the decision and the subsequent monitoring. Because the prudence of an investment is not to be determined in isolation but in the context of the overall portfolio, I believe good recordkeeping can provide a committee's strongest defense. I suspect many committees, however, are not as careful about this as they should be.

We have talked continually about the importance of having an *adviser*. But what should cause us to lose confidence in our *adviser*? There are two basic things an *adviser* should do for us:

1. Help us develop our Investment Policy and our Policy Asset Allocation (including our Benchmark Portfolio).

2. Recommend whom to hire as *investment managers* and when to terminate a *manager*.

   The second function is easiest to quantify. If over a period of three to five years our actual returns have not equaled or exceeded our Benchmark Portfolio, that would be evidence that the *adviser's* recommendations of *managers* have not been particularly good.

   The first function is harder to quantify except in the long term. If our *adviser* has led us to a widely diversified portfolio, our Benchmark Portfolio might underperform more conventional portfolios during intervals when conventional asset classes such as large U.S. stocks and investment grade bonds have outperformed most other asset classes. This, however, would probably not be a time to switch *advisers*.

   On the other hand, if we have not approved most of our *adviser's* recommendations, how can we hold our *adviser* accountable? Perhaps it is our own committee's approach that we should be modifying.

   Finally, a number one function of any *adviser*, in my opinion, is to give us continuing investment education. If the *adviser* is not doing that, or if we cannot achieve a rapport with our *adviser*, perhaps it is time to consider a change.

Italicized words, as used in this book:

> *adviser*   Investment staff, consultant, or other source of investment expertise to an investment committee.
>
> *fund*   Investment fund.
>
> *investment fund*   Our endowment fund, foundation, or pension fund.
>
> *investment manager*   Investment manager or commingled fund such as a mutual fund.
>
> *manager*   Investment manager.

12(b)(1) fees   Fees charged by a mutual fund to cover advertising and promotional expenses.

401(k) plan   A defined-contribution pension plan offered by many corporations.

aggregate volatility   The volatility of a total portfolio, as opposed to the volatility of individual securities, individual managers, or individual asset classes.

alpha   Technically, the risk-adjusted return on a security or a portfolio in excess of its benchmark. In common parlance, the simple difference between a portfolio's return and that of its benchmark.

alternative asset classes   Asset classes other than traditional asset classes such as stocks and bonds.

arbitrage programs   Programs that are both long and short, such as long security A and short security B, so that results depend entirely on the difference in return between securities A and B.

asset class   A category of assets, such as large U.S. stocks, or high-yield bonds, or venture capital.

asset/liability studies   Studies based on (a) assumptions about the future performance of specific asset classes and (b) projected liabilities of a pension fund, to determine an optimal asset allocation.

back-loaded mutual funds   Mutual funds that charge a fee when an investor sells the mutual fund.

bell curve   A normal frequency curve, a distribution curve that is symmetrical on both sides of the median.

benchmark   A basis of comparison for the investment return of an *investment manager* or for an overall portfolio.

benchmark portfolio A portfolio of asset classes (with a benchmark, usually an index, identified for each asset class) whose theoretical return serves as the benchmark for an *investment fund*.

benchmark risk The risk that an *investment manager* or a *fund* may deviate materially from its benchmark.

beta A measure of the volatility or a stock or a portfolio relative to a benchmark index (such as the S&P 500). A beta of more than 1 means more volatile than an index, a beta of less than 1 means less volatile.

board-designated endowment Money designated by an organization's board of directors (rather than the donor) to be treated as endowment.

book value The price that was paid for an investment.

buy-in funds Private investment funds that invest directly in private shares of an established company.

buy-out funds Private investment funds that purchase all outstanding shares of a company.

capitalization of a stock The number of a company's shares outstanding (or available for trading) times the price of its stock.

capitalization-weighted index A securities index that weights each security in direct proportion to its capitalization.

CEO (chief executive officer) of a *fund* The chief officer heading the staff of an investment *fund*.

certificate of deposit A deposit with a bank of a specific amount of money for a specific time at a specific rate of interest.

commingled fund A fund in which two or more clients invest. Mutual funds, group trusts, and most limited partnerships are common examples.

commodity future For example, a contract to buy an amount of corn by a specific date at a specific price. There are 22 or more listed commodity futures, including grains, foreign exchange, and petroleum products.

convertible arbitrage A program that buys convertible securities and sells short the stocks into which those securities are convertible.

correlation A statistical term measuring the amount of similarity between the volatilities of any two indexes, individual securities, or investment portfolios.

custodian The organization that holds and reports on the assets of an *investment fund*.

defined-benefit pension plan A pension plan where the benefit is not impacted by whether investment returns are good or bad.

defined-contribution pension plan A pension plan, such as a 401(k) plan, where the employee bears the entire risk or opportunity of investment results.

derivative A security such as a convertible bond or futures contract whose market value is derived all or partly from a different security. Examples of derivatives are listed on pages 28–29.

distressed securities Securities of a company that is in or heading toward bankruptcy.

diversification Assembling a portfolio of securities that fluctuate in value differently from one another.

diversifiable risk   Volatility that can be eliminated through diversification.

diversification benefit   The reduction in volatility or increase in return that can be gained through the diversification of a portfolio.

dividend yield   A stock's dividend as a percent of its market value.

dollar-weighted return   Internal rate of return, the average percent return on every dollar that was invested over an interval of time.

donor-designated endowment   Money designated by its donor to be treated as endowment.

duration   Duration is a measure of the average amount of time until we receive our returns on an investment, including both interest and principal payments.

efficient frontier   Given assumptions for the return, volatility, and correlation of each asset class, the Efficient Frontier is a graph showing the highest return that can be achieved at every level of portfolio volatility.

emerging markets   Stock and bond markets of the less developed countries of the world.

EPS (earnings per share)   The net earnings of a company divided by the number of its outstanding shares.

ERISA (the Employee Retirement Income Security Act)   The U.S. law that governs all private pension plans in the country.

fiduciary   A person in a special position of trust and responsibility for an *investment fund*.

fixed income   Bonds and cash equivalents, whose principal and interest payments are fixed.

foreign exchange risk   The risk of losing money because of the reduced value of foreign currencies.

forward (forward contract)   An agreement to buy (or sell) a security at some future date at a price agreed upon today.

front-loaded mutual fund   A mutual fund that deducts a sales charge from a purchase of that fund.

funding ratio   The ratio of (a) the market value of a pension fund to (b) the present value of the liabilities of that pension fund.

future (future contract)   An agreement to pay or receive, until some future date, the change in price of a particular security or an index.

FX (foreign exchange)   Foreign currencies.

GDP/GNP   Gross Domestic Product and Gross National Product are two measures of the size of a nation's economy.

growth stocks   Stocks with higher growth rates in earnings per share.

hedge   An investment that reduces the risk of another investment.

hedge funds   A term designating a broad range of funds that make both long and short investments, sometimes using a variety of derivatives.

high-grade bonds   Bonds with high quality ratings.

high-yield bonds   Bonds with lower quality ratings, once known as "junk bonds."

illiquid assets   Assets that cannot be readily sold or otherwise converted to cash, usually for at least a year and perhaps for many years.

Imputed Income method   A method for determining the amount of income to be paid annually by an endowment fund to its sponsor. Also called the Total Return method.

index (a securities index)   A measure of the investment return on an asset class.

index funds   An investment fund that is designed to replicate as closely as possible the return on a particular index; for example, an S&P 500 index fund.

inflation-linked bonds   Bonds whose interest rate is stated in real terms—in percentage points exceeding the inflation rate.

in-house management   Management of all or a portion of a *fund's* investments by its internal staff.

interest rate arbitrage   Buying a fixed income security and selling short a different fixed income security.

internal rate of return (IRR)   The average percent return on every dollar that was invested over an interval of time; a dollar-weighted rate of return.

investment-grade bonds   Bonds with high quality ratings, usually BBB and above.

Investment Policies   An organization's written policies relative to the investment of its *fund*.

IRA (Individual Retirement Account)   An individual's personal taxfree investment fund.

LBO (leveraged buyout)   The purchase of an entire company through the significant use of borrowed money.

leverage   Investing with the use of borrowed money or credit.

liabilities of a pension fund   The value of promises made to the participants in a pension plan, usually the present value of those promises.

LIBOR   The London interbank offered rate, generally used as the interest rate assumed implicitly in the pricing of futures.

liquid assets   Assets that can be sold or otherwise can be converted to cash in less than a year.

long/short investments   Investments that are both long and short, such as buying security A (long) and borrowing and selling security B (short), so that results depend entirely on the difference in return between securities A and B.

market-neutral investments   Investments whose volatility has a very low correlation with the volatility of the stock and bond markets.

market value   The price at which an investment could be sold at any given time.

maverick risk   The perceived risk in making investments that are different from those of one's peers.

median   The midpoint of a distribution, with half above and half below.

merger & acquisition (M&A) arbitrage   The purchase of stock in a company that is expected to be acquired and the short sale of stock in the acquiring company.

micro stocks   The smallest stocks, such as (in the U.S.) stocks smaller than those included in the Russell 2000 index.

mid-cap stocks   Mid-size stocks, such as (in the U.S.) stocks larger than those included in the Russell 2000 index, but excluding the largest stocks.

money market mutual funds   Mutual funds that invest in fixed income securities shorter than one year in maturity, funds whose price is not expected to fluctuate.

Monte Carlo probability methods   Random number generators whose output is intended to fit a normal probability curve.

net returns   Investment returns that are net of all fees and expenses.

no-load mutual funds   Mutual funds that do not make a sales charge when the investor buys or sells its shares.

opportunity cost   The return that a *fund* could have made if it had made an investment that it didn't make.

Operating Policies   An organization's written policies relative to the operation of its investment committee.

options   The right, but not the obligation, to buy a security from (or sell a security to) a particular party at a given price by a given date.

PBGC (Pension Benefit Guarantee Corporation)   A U.S. government agency that insures the payment of pension benefits up to a certain benefit level in the event that a private pension plan is terminated and can't come up with the money to meet its promises.

Policy Asset Allocation   The target asset allocation that an organization has established in its Investment Policies.

portable alpha   Investing in an index fund through index futures , and then investing the cash that isn't used for collateral in a market-neutral investment program.

portfolio   All of the securities held by an *investment fund*.

predictive value   The extent a *manager's* past performance may provide some indication of that manager's future performance. See pages 107–110.

price/earnings ratio   The ratio of a stock's price to its earnings per share.

private investments   Investments that are not sold publicly.

proxy   The voting on issues to be decided at a stockholder's meeting.

quantitative managers   Managers who develop and rely on mathematical algorithms to determine the transactions to be made in managing an investment portfolio.

quartile   One-quarter of a distribution, for example the top 25% or the bottom 25%.

real return   Investment return in excess of inflation.

realized capital gain   The change in price of an investment from the time it was purchased to the time it was sold.

rebalancing   Transactions that bring a portfolio's asset allocation closer to the *investment fund's* Policy Asset Allocation.

reinvested dividends   Dividends paid by a stock that are used to buy more shares of that stock. For example, a total return index assumes that all dividends are reinvested.

REITs (real estate investment trusts)   Common stocks of companies that invest in real estate, but which—instead of paying corporate income tax—pass their income tax liability on to their shareholders.

restricted endowment   Endowment money that the donor restricted for a special purpose.

risk   The probability of losing money, or that the value of our investment will go down. For a portfolio of investments, risk is often defined as volatility, which over long intervals tends to encompass most individual risks.

risk-adjusted return   Return-on-investment adjusted for its volatility over time, with a volatile investment requiring a higher return and vice versa.

securities   Evidence of ownership or debt, such as stocks or bonds.

separate accounts   A portfolio that is held for only one investor. (Insurance companies, however, use "separate accounts" to denote a portfolio held for one or more investors that is valued for those investors at market value.)

Sharpe Ratio   A measure of risk-adjusted return: specifically, an investment's rate of return in excess of the T-bill rate, divided by the investment's standard deviation.

short selling   Borrowing a security and then selling it.

short-term investment fund (STIF)   A money market fund provided by a bank for investment clients for whom the bank serves as custodian.

small stocks   Stocks with relatively low capitalization, sometimes measured by the Russell 2000 index.

social investing   Overlaying a *fund's* investment objectives with a set of social goals that constrain the *fund* from investing in certain kinds of companies or that encourage it to invest in certain other kinds of companies.

standard deviation   A measure of volatility of the return on a security or a portfolio.

structured note   A private financial agreement between two parties relating to the securities markets.

style   The manner in which a *manager* invests, such as in small, medium, or large stocks, or in growth stocks or value stocks.

swap   An agreement between two parties to pay or receive, until some future time, the difference in return between one party's portfolio (or an index) and the counterparty's portfolio (or an index).

systematic risk   The portion of a security's volatility that is highly correlated with all or a portion of the market; for example, the portion of a stock's volatility that is highly correlated with the overall stock market or with other stocks in its own industry.

tactical asset allocation   A strategy of moving investments between different asset classes (such as between stocks and bonds), depending on which seems more attractive at the time. Such strategies are typically driven by quantitative models.

Target Asset Allocation   See Policy Asset Allocation.

time diversification   Purchasing investments in an asset class in multiple different years.

time horizon   The time between when one makes an investment and when one will need to use the money for other purposes.

time-weighted return   The compound annual growth rate of a dollar that was in a portfolio from the beginning of an interval to the end of that interval. The portfolio's performance in each unit of time is given equal weight.

TIPS (Treasury Inflation-Protected Securities)   Inflation-linked bonds issued by the U.S. government.

total return   The investment return on a security or a portfolio that includes income (such as dividends and interest) and capital gains (whether realized or not), net of all fees and expenses.

total return index   A securities index that assumes that all dividends are reinvested in the issuing company's stock.

Total Return method   See Imputed Income method.

track record   The historical investment performance of a *manager*.

transaction costs   The total costs involved in buying or selling a security, including both brokerage commissions and market impact costs.

Treasury bill (T-bill)   A short-term loan to the U.S. government.

TSE 300   The leading index of Canadian stocks.

unrealized capital gain   The change in price of an investment from the time it was purchased to its present market value.

value stocks   Stocks with lower price-to-book-value ratios.

venture capital   Private corporate investments, especially in start-up companies.

volatility   Fluctuation in the market value of a security or a portfolio.

wealth   The total market value of a portfolio at any given time.

withdrawal from a *fund*   The cash payment by an *investment fund* to its sponsor or to its plan participants.

Wilshire 500 index   A capitalization-weighted index of virtually all stocks traded in the U.S., including foreign stocks listed on U.S. exchanges.

Bibliography

*Ambachtsheer, Keith P., and D. Don Ezra. *Pension Fund Excellence*. John Wiley & Sons, Inc., 1998.

Bernstein, Peter L. *Against the Gods: The Remarkable Story of Risk*. John Wiley & Sons, Inc., 1998.

Bernstein, William J. *The Four Pillars of Investing: Lessons for Building a Winning Portfolio*. McGraw-Hill, 2002.

*Bernstein, William J. *The Intelligent Asset Allocator: How to Build Your Portfolio to Maximize Returns and Minimize Risk*. McGraw-Hill, 2000.

Bogle, John C. *Common Sense on Mutual Funds: New Imperatives for the Intelligent Investor*. John Wiley & Sons, Inc., 2000.

Chancellor, Edward. *Devil Take the Hindmost*. Plume, 2000.

Clowes, Michael J. *The Money Flood: How Pension Funds Revolutionized Investing*. John Wiley & Sons, Inc., 2000.

Crerend, William J. *Fundamentals of Hedge Fund Investing: A Professional Investor's Guide*. McGraw-Hill, 1998.

*Ellis, Charles. *Winning the Loser's Game: Timeless Strategies for Successful Investing*. McGraw-Hill Professional Publishing, 2000.

*Ibbotson Associates. *2002 Yearbook: Market Results for 1926–2001*. Ibbotson Associates, 2002.

Lowenstein, Roger. *When Genius Failed: The Rise and Fall of Long-Term Capital Management*. Random House, 2000.

MacKay, Charles, and Andrew Tobias. *Extraordinary Popular Delusions & the Madness of Crowds*, Crown Pub, 1995.

Malkiel, Burton Gordon. *A Random Walk Down Wall Street*. 7th Ed. W. W. Norton & Company, 2000.

Michaud, Richard O. *Efficient Asset Management*. Harvard Business School Press, 1998.

Sherden, William A. *The Fortune Sellers*. John Wiley & Sons, Inc., 1998.

*Swenson, David F. *Pioneering Portfolio Management*. The Free Press, 2000.

*Tanous, Peter J. *Investment Gurus*. New York Institute of Finance, 1997.

*Trone, Donald B., Mark A. Rickloff, J. Richard Lynch, and Andrew T. Frommeyer. *Prudent Investment Practices: A Handbook for Investment Fiduciaries*. Center for Fiduciary Studies, 2004.

*Yoder, Jay A. *Endowment Management: A Practical Guide*. Association of Governing Boards of Universities and Colleges, 2004.

---

*Books referenced in the footnotes.

Index

About the Author

Rusty Olson, a consultant on institutional investing, retired in 2000 as Director of Pension Investments, Worldwide, for Eastman Kodak Company. Olson had overseen Kodak's pension funds since 1972. Over the 1980s and 1990s (and through 2003), Kodak's pension fund was one of the best performing pension funds in the United States. Kodak made contributions to its pension fund in only two of the 22 years, 1983–2004, and as of year-end 2003 Kodak's was one of few corporate pension funds that was essentially fully funded. Olson was named one of America's nine best pension officers by *Institutional Investor* magazine in 1987 and was Investment Management Institute's first "Plan Sponsor of the Year" in 1993.

Olson began serving on an endowment investment committee in 1972 and remains a member of half a dozen endowment investment committees with whom he has served for 15 to 20 years.

He holds a B.A. degree in journalism from Rutgers University and an M.B.A. from the Harvard Business School.

Olson is the author of:

- *The School of Hard Knocks: The Evolution of Kodak's Pension Investment Management* (Rochester Institute of Technology's Cary Graphic Arts Press, 2005)
- *Investing in Pension Funds and Endowments: Tools and Guidelines for the New Independent Fiduciary* (McGraw-Hill, 2003)
- *The Independent Fiduciary: Investing for Pension Funds and Endowment Funds* (John Wiley & Sons, 1999)

The web site for his books is: *www.theindependentfiduciary.com.*